My Sister Helped Me Heal:
The Power of Kingdom Sisterhood

Visionary Chavon Anette

My Sister Helped Me Heal:
The Power of Kingdom Sisterhood

Copyright © 2022 by Chavon Thomas
ISBN: 978-0-578-38004-9

Cover Design: iambiancabrown.com

Printed in the USA:
All rights reserved. No part of this book may be reproduced or used in any manner without written permission of the copyright owner except for the use of quotations in a book review. For more information, address: www.chavonanette.com

Dedication:

To all The Sisters Around the World who Helped Their Sisters Heal and the ones who God is about to send someone your way.

Table of Contents

Section 1	9
Introduction	
To the Healing of Hearts	11
Chapter 1	
My Sister is NOT My Enemy1 by Kiyanni Bryan	13
Chapter 2	
She didn't Know What She Carried Until… by Nakia Harris	17
Chapter 3	
Why Are You Here? by Dr. Karen Hills Pruden	22
Chapter 4	
Teach Me to Pray by Ebony Cherry	26
Chapter 5	
Uprooting The Seeds by Tienisha Earl	31
Chapter 6	
Sisterhood Helped Me Heal by Domonique Peele	35
Chapter 7	
Candy Jar Sister Testimony by Lady Candace L. Green	39
Chapter 8	
My Sister Helped Me Heal by Dr. Charlene Winley	43
Chapter 9	
My Plan Didn't Work by Jessica Simmons	47
Chapter 10	
A Divine Meet-up by Pastor Paulette Harper	51

SECTION 2   57

CHAPTER 11
I am a Woman of Life by Lakia Perez   59

CHAPTER 12
Darkness didn't Stop my Healing by Ronjeanna Unorthodox Certified Wellness Coach   63

CHAPTER 13
Hidden in insecurity to walking in purpose confidently by Antoinette Hines   68

CHAPTER 14
The Angel that Helped Me Heal by Michelle Franklin   72

CHAPTER 15
Covered by Dr. Charlene Bell   76

CHAPTER 16
They (She) helped me find ME! by Alexis Ganier   80

CHAPTER 17
A Mother's Love by Apostle Tina M. Beatty   84

CHAPTER 18
Down but Not Out by Melissa L. Bell   88

CHAPTER 19
The Drop Could Have Killed Me But God by Shelia Cook   92

CHAPTER 20
Ode to My Sisters by Tamia Copeland   96

EPILOGUE
This is Just Our Beginning   101

Foreword

Perhaps this is what this season is all about: Trusting in the unknowns, Finding gold in the little things, Trading fear of what's uncertain for freedom to thrive within...Choose JOY!

But how can it be done?

The Broken Fragments of a hurting heart are like the pieces of a glass that's been shattered on the floor.

A few days ago, I knocked over a glass of water and the glass shattered into many pieces, the jagged edges of the glass were literally everywhere on my floor!

I immediately cleaned up the glass, diligently searching for the fine pieces that are so hard to see, because even the tiniest shard of glass left on the ground can cut and hurt the paws of my puppy, my baby girl's feet or even my own.

Well, two days later as I was walking barefoot into my living room, I immediately stepped on a sharp object. The residue from the glass was so fine, I couldn't see it, but I felt it, as it pierced my skin.

If I could've seen the glass, I could have prevented the pain from hurting me.

Even though I was very careful the other day and had taken my time to clean up the broken glass, there were still some pieces I couldn't see.

This is what came to me from this experience:

When the broken pieces of hurt aren't clear anymore because they're being overshadowed and it affects your clarity and how you see, what do you do? What can you do?

Let's talk about your healing. As these ladies share their personal stories, their highs and lows, I encourage you to allow yourself to feel so that you can heal allow the Lord to do a deep work in you. You're worth a fight!

Psalm 34:4
I sought the LORD, and he answered me; he delivered me from all my fears.

This is what I know to be true, healing is a daily process.
It's A JOURNEY.
Deliverance and healing don't always happen overnight.
It's not a sweep you up and done and nothing else to worry about.
- You *have to* make an intentional daily choice to use your tools.
- You *have to* choose to face the things that you're going through, to sit with it and look at the hurt.
- You *have to* accept that it may take longer than you want it to, and decide--you will not quit.

In this way you too will experience, #triumphovertrauma. May the stories of these women take the "Shame off you."™

Kristal Klear
Founder of Rock, Paper, Scissors Foundation

Section 1

INTRODUCTION

To the Healing of Hearts

"Look at her"- my eyes meet my friend- "I support and love you."

"Look at her"- my eyes shift to my next friend- "I support and love you."

"Look at her"- my eyes turn to my other friend- "I support and love you."

"Look at me"- my eyes are at my friend creating this moment- "I support and love you."

It was moments before I would speak for my first in-person event. God led my friend Kiyanni Bryan to instruct me to turn and look at all my sisters in the back room with me - Lakia Perez, Ciara Mason, Melissa Daughtry, and herself, and allow them to say those words to me. With tears rolling down my eyes, the reality of their words sinking in brought me to a new level of freedom and deliverance.

It can weigh on you when you have had to manage the fights of ministry and fights in your personal life. It never means quitting or giving up, but with the right people around you, it still means making sure you position yourself to heal in the areas where you have been wounded.

This was not the first time God sent women, better yet sisters, my way to help me heal. However, in a season where acceleration was happening for a purpose in my life, this moment was required because on the other side of the joy was the warfare that was trying to get me to abort purpose.

My Sister Helped Me Heal was a title God gave me in 2021. I immediately got excited because I knew I could write about this. Kingdom sisterhood has been so vital in my life. It especially surprised me when He said, "It will not just be your story, but this book will be for many women to join together."

As you flip the pages of this book, you are in for stories that may trouble you, cause you to cry, or relate to your own life, but this book is also a message of Hope.

We all have been in seasons of our lives where challenges made us feel like attaining our goals was an impossible feat. Nevertheless, with God and divine assigned people in our lives, we can see the light peeping through the clouds.

Kingdom sisterhood turned my life around for the better. Allowing the right people in truly saved my life. My life shifted for the better socially and emotionally as a CEO and as a minister of the gospel.

The best part about this book is that you will find that this is not something great that God just did for me, but he is doing it for all of us if we are willing to open our hearts again.

Women can collaborate instead of competing and love instead of envy. Women can hold each other up while also holding each other accountable. Women can support other women's businesses and trust that they will receive support in turn. Women can share their highs and lows and trust the whole world won't know.

This is the Power of Kingdom sisterhood!!!

Chapter 1

My Sister is NOT My Enemy

-Kiyanni Bryan

Growing up in South Bronx, New York, with my family in the projects, I was raised by the majority of women. A host of loving aunties, grandaunts, female cousins, my mother, and grandmother. My thought process about women and the base of my understanding of sister relationships was molded by the loving and supportive family environment that I was groomed in.

Sisterhood represented a "safe place" to be yourself. I learned over time that these relationships don't always turn out the way we think. Like many of you, I have experienced the bitter taste of betrayal and jealousy by women I deemed sisters and even one of my biological sisters. It was traumatizing, to say the least, and changed my view on sister relationships. My experiences with jealousy, envy, two-faced, backbiting, betrayal, and lack of loyalty caused disappointment and despair that hit so hard I could barely speak, but what was worse is that it builds a defensive guard to the heart that can hinder my growth.

The truth is that some of those experiences caused me to stop trusting women, and I then gravitated to the fellas. The thinking was men aren't petty, they aren't bitter, they don't come with half the headache, and I definitely wouldn't have to worry about petty and conniving behaviors. I'm safe, right? Or, I think. Relationships are real people with real-life issues, and although we would like to think that those behavior patterns are gender-based, it is simply not true because it's about the heart condition.

The Lord taught me how to sift through my situations to determine the root. God did not orchestrate some of the relationships I had. I had sisters with toxic bonds such as pain, bad character traits, affliction in similar areas, and bad motives. The same toxic behavior that joined us ended us. You should always exercise wisdom in your relationships, but not paranoia to think that women can't be trusted. Let God deal with the thing that caused that frame of thinking so that you don't miss out on opportunities that are directly connected to sisters.

To date, one of my best friends was a rare situation of a sisterhood that was built. After a season of bad friendships, or people who just didn't understand who I was and all that God was grooming me to be, I met my sister. There was a woman that I had known for years at a church I used to attend, but we didn't have a relationship. Over the years, I would see her at conferences before I joined that ministry, and we ended up being on the prophetic ministry team together. She was beautiful! She looked like a doll baby to me and was very down to earth. All I knew about her was that she was nice, kept to herself, could sing, and was on the same dance ministry I later joined. One bible study night, the Lord began to speak to me about her, and then she walked into the church. I was led to sit next to her, and we both could feel the Lord's presence. She said that she was led to connect with me, and from that night, we exchanged numbers and GOD built that sisterhood.

Never had I seen the Lord put together a friendship like the way this happened. Now, five years later, she is one of my best friends. We have co-labored together and have overcome hurdles as sisters. She showed me that all women aren't the same, and there isn't always a hidden agenda. I experienced immeasurable amounts of healing through our sisterhood by having an accountable person to walk through the bad and ugly with. Deliverance can be very messy, and we have held hands through the process of ensuring each other's healing. My sister literally HELPED ME HEAL.

Over the years, the Lord has sent me some of the most loving, and trusting women that I have been able to collaborate, partner, work with, coach, minister alongside, and build covenant friendships with. These women are from all walks of life, some with different beliefs, diverse in nature and different circles. These women have spoken life into me that has resurrected dead places, places of hurt that I thought had NO Point of Return.

My sisters helped me heal by being the safe space and place for me to be WHO I AM, with vulnerability and no judgment. They loved me, covered me, honored me, warred for me, poured into me, sacrificed for me, stood in the GAP for me, and LOVED me with all purity. We need safe places to heal, and it is actually impossible to heal when you feel unsafe. I am enjoying the journey and have experienced healing internally and subsequently externally. There are no lone rangers in the body of Christ, and although I have close male friends relationships, nothing beats the girls' trips, sleepovers, and dinners. (Smiles) Love covers and community heals.

Relationships carry destiny moves; it is a MUST to let God deal with your pain points. I used to go as far as to say, "I don't trust women; they got too much going on." I had no idea that was a form of self-rejection and that thinking would block friendships. I had to relearn the beauty that comes with sisters and just let some things go. It is hard to allow someone to be a part of your healing process if your reflex response to them is that they have the potential to harm you.

Your sister is one of your leading intercessors. They help you heal your life and assist in the process of restoring you. The enemy wars against women in relationships, women supporting each other, and women having tight bonds that form inner safety circles. When we unite, you know what we are capable of, so let your sister know, 'I see you, I love you, I support you because I AM YOU.'

Bio

Kiyanni B. is an Author, Life Strategist, Transformational Speaker, Publisher, and Next Level Coach specializing in helping leaders impact in the area of their identity and THRIVE in kingdom life and business. She engages them in a process where she creates solutions and strategies that enable them to overcome their greatest obstacles with clarity, implementation, and accountability.

She is the owner of Kiyanni Impacts LLC, a consultancy that offers personal life and business coaching services, as well as small business corporate consulting services in the area of business startup, project management, office operations, employee relations, business strategy, branding, and marketing.

Kiyanni is the founder of Write It Out Publishing LLC, where she assists authors with the birthing of their vision of being an author, setting up their business, and creating impactful messages that change the world, one reader, at a time.

Chapter 2

She didn't Know What She Carried Until...

- Nakia Harris

Growing up wasn't easy for me, but I managed. I grew up in church, knew how to pray at an early age, and never had a lot of friends. In fact, I was very smart, very sneaky, and very promiscuous. I never really wanted to hang out with people my age, and females were not a good look for good company. I lost my virginity at an early age; let's just say I should have still been playing with dolls. I remember that every day after school, I had to see Eugene because we had to "goose," and it would be fun. We were goosing, and he was my first. I mastered it the first time, and after that, it was an open door to sexual perversions and heartaches that I was not prepared for.

Now, I had both my parents in the home, and while things were a struggle for us, my parents managed to give their best and do their best with what they had, especially my mother. I had a present father, but he was absent in the prominent areas of love, affection, and an example of letting me know what to expect in a man. I didn't know what to look for, even what love from a man felt like, so when it happened, what I thought was real and right, turned out to be wrong and dysfunctional. It was damaging and demise, but I went for it anyway because I didn't know what I carried.

WHAT SHE WAS CARRYING WAS TOO HEAVY, SO SHE DROPPED IT

By now, the question becomes, what did she carry? Well, by 14, I was playing with the big dogs, and I met this guy. I knew of him; he was charming and way older than me. We talked one day, and he asked me if he could wash his hands. I thought it was nothing, so I let him in, and from there, he took full advantage of the situation, me, and when he was finished, the aftereffects changed my life. I carried guilt, fault, shame, humiliation, and I was silenced in anger. In that very moment, I stopped trusting a man, I stopped trusting God, and trouble was in my future.

I got caught up with feeling less than, so I got in relationships that resemble such things. I left home at 18. Upon leaving, that was the first time I heard my father say I love you, and it crushed me. I got married at 19, had a daughter, and she was the highlight of my life. I then had a son. I thought being married was the best thing until the verbal abuse started, then physical and then sexual, and next would be generational curses and demonic strongholds. Out of infidelity, I had another daughter.

I lived overseas for some time and met another man who would take me places sexually and taught me the meaning of exploring my mind, body, and soul. I met three female officers over there that God sent to deliver me out of what they saw was a downward spiral. I returned to the states, got a divorce, and met another man who would be controlling, possessive, and determined to be my soul tie. Being connected to this man introduced me to my sister and friend that would become a prayer warrior for my inner healing. She knew what I carried, and her prayers were helping me to discover what I carried to break free.

Trained (concealed to carry and now armed and ready)

It was good that I was afflicted with so much nonsense. At a young age, I carried so many emotions. When I became an adult, those emotions intensified into spirits. Men rejected me, and I rejected God because my earthly authority of a man was mishandled, misrepresented, and misunderstood. This caused me to present myself in misleading roles that looked like love and superiority, but it was perverse and deception at best.

With all that I had going on, God called me into ministry to be and do greater than what appeared to be. All of these experiences that was God taking me through was intensive care. It got to the point that I was so crippled and so damaged, I couldn't parent, I lost everything, I was living pillow to post until I got to place of full surrender. I was dead emotionally and gasping for air. At that moment, God began filling in the gap and the holes that had been bruised, battered, and shaken.

God was committed and concerned about what would be an appointed time. Appointed time meant that I had to undergo pruning, processing, and training from trial and error. It's the experience that creates the lesson for the story to be told. I didn't want to go through the process of healing the hurting and not remembering, and most importantly, I didn't want to forgive. I didn't want to face that I carried the very anointing of God, and that is what these men were attracted to. I had to forgive myself and then the others. I had to forgive this man and that man and this illicit act of deception. I had to forgive myself for not valuing what I carried and for distorting God's objective for a greater me. I learned, I survived, and God concealed what I carried then and now, for he wants to release what I carry.

KNOW WHAT YOU CARRY AND BE READY TO USE IT

God was showing me that through all these stressful casualties, what I considered traumatic was the need for me to be conscious and deliberate. These men came with a purpose to destroy and infect me with persecution, humiliation, retaliation, unforgiveness, and shame. These men were instruments to try to taint the anointing. I found it ironic that God was showing me that these men were never attracted to me, yet I still wanted to give them something valuable. I wanted to give all of me, not knowing that all of me also meant carrying the weight of his glory.

If we leave things up to ourselves to figure it all, we will find enough reasons to disqualify what God has created, designed, drafted, and stamped as a prerequisite. In all that I had experienced and still experiencing, I found that I am qualified to carry, complete, and release what looks and seems impossible. I carry the authority, the audacity, and the authenticity of until. I know now what I carry is powerful, important, and impactful. What was being done was a transformation for what the next phase.

Bio

Nakia is a Veteran, a mother, avid speaker, mentor, and educator. She is a connector of resources and enthusiastic about prison reformation and educating the minds of young adults. After being called into ministry, Nakia became a vessel for strategic foresight and an intercessor. Nakia is the founder of Project C.H.A.N.G.E Inc., committed to "Cultivating a Culture of Change."

In this season, God is using her voice not only to be a Change Agent for Kingdom assignments but expand her creativity as a Change Coach. In her spare time, Nakia empowers women in her Women's group called Women of the NOW- New Opportunities of Wisdom, and her Teen Girls Club at School called Next level conversations. Her favorite saying is, "The only thing constant is change; if that be true, you're constantly evolving the change in you."

Nakia is a native of Maryland but currently resides in Norfolk, Virginia.

Chapter 3

Why Are You Here?

- Dr. Karen Hills Pruden

Watching someone battle cancer with chemotherapy and blood transfusions can drain you. I had to be optimistic when my eyes were telling me Robert was dying. So, I put on a brave smile and joked a lot. My job was to help him feel better.

It was crazy that Robert was even diagnosed with cancer. I was unaware that there were so many forms of cancer. I knew of breast and lung cancer. Those were the cancers that had television commercials and news segments. Breast cancer even has its own month, October.

Robert was diagnosed with a form of cancer that normally attacks children. Robert was in his thirties. So, yes, it was surprising that he would be diagnosed with that form of cancer. He did not smoke. He was losing weight at the time of his diagnosis. Robert was previously 250 pounds.

He was losing weight when his body began to change drastically. The weight came off so fast it scared him. He went to the doctor and found out that his weight loss was being assisted by something that had invaded his body, cancer.

When Robert was diagnosed with cancer, we had recently parted ways. We dated for eight years. I felt it was time for marriage, but he wanted to wait. We separated. A phone call from one of my girlfriends alerted me that he was in the hospital. She knew how I felt about him. I am forever grateful for that phone call.

I immediately went to the hospital to see him. When I entered the room and he saw it was me, he would not even look at me. He asked me, 'Why are you here?" I was crushed. I left quickly. I called the friend who alerted me of his hospital admission and told her how he treated me. She listened and calmly said, "He probably does not want you to see him like that. I think he was happy you came. Go Back." I went back the next day. I am forever grateful for her encouragement.

Same response the next day, he turned away from my direction. Instead of leaving, I sat in the chair in the room. After a few hours of different people coming in and out of the room, he turned in my direction and repeated his question, "Why are you here?" I responded because my friend told me you were sick. I want to be here. He said, "Well, you can leave." I did not respond. I did not leave, either. My friend and I had already discussed this possible scenario.

The doctors gave him two months to live. As we talked, Robert shared that he did not want me to see him like that. The cancer had morphed him into a totally different person. He did not look like his former self.

However, his mind and his sense of humor were intact. We rekindled our relationship. One day on the way to chemotherapy, we stopped by the jeweler. He purchased me another engagement ring. This time we set a wedding date. He regretted that he hesitated about something that was so important to me. Deposits were paid, and the invitations were mailed. We planned a wedding that we always knew we would have.

When I grew tired of crying in the bathroom where Robert could not see me, I called my girlfriends. We would eat and recall all the crazy escapades of Robert and me. They were right beside me most of those times, anyway.

One morning, Robert woke me up very early. I slept in a neighboring chair so that he could be comfortable in the bed. He whispered, "Call the ambulance." He was calm. I called and then asked him why. He said he was having problems breathing. As we waited for the doctor in the emergency room, Robert laid his head on my shoulder. I was talking, trying to distract him from whatever could be going on with him medically. I noticed he was no longer engaging. I raised his head. His eyes were open, but he was not responding. I called for someone. The nurse came in and checked his pulse. Fluid had accumulated around Robert's heart. He was pronounced dead.

I walked into the lobby and informed his family of his death. Only one person was allowed in the room. They decided I should go back with him. I quickly exited the hospital. I could feel the tears and weight of the entire experience rising in my chest.

Tears began to roll down my face as I picked up my speed to get to my car before I exploded with emotions. I could hear footsteps behind me. As my hand reached for the car door, I heard my name being yelled in unison. The voices were familiar. They were my closest girlfriends. They had been sitting in the lobby to support me. Robert lived for eight months after his diagnosis. He died two weeks before our wedding.

There is no greater relationship than one where you can be your authentic self and be truly accepted. I have been fortunate over my life to come across women at various times who have served as my counselor, voice of reason, and confidante. Some relationships started because we had a common interest. Maybe we worked together or were casual acquaintances that evolved into lifelong relationships. In some cases, I became closer to some of my female friends than I was to my very own sister.

As we navigate life, we find ourselves in various situations where we lean on one another for assistance. Reciprocity is not something you think about in relationships. However, it seems to happen when you interact with the same individuals for an extended period. I could not have made it through that experience without my closest girlfriends. I am grateful I was with Robert when he took his last breath.

My Sister Helped Me Heal:

Bio

Dr. Karen Hills Pruden is the *C-Suite Career Elevation Expert* for women seeking senior leadership. She has decades of experience in influencing others through global speaking, coaching, workshops, and authoring bestselling books. Dr. Pruden works as a Chief Human Resource Officer for a Virginia university, Pruden Global Business Solutions Consulting (CEO), Sister Leaders Conference (CEO), and the Creator/Host of *Leadership Is Served,* an international television show that facilitates uncensored, leader-to-leader conversations. Dr. Pruden has been interviewed on *Roland Martin Unfiltered,* ABC, NBC, CBS affiliates and national radio stations. She has been a keynote speaker on many international stages.

Drkarenhillspruden.com

Chapter 4

Teach Me to Pray

- Ebony Cherry

The last time I remember things being "normal" was when I was five. We had just moved into our three-bedroom apartment. I can remember wanting to be successful from the beginning. Sick or well, rainy or sunny, cold or hot, I was going to school. School came easily for me, and I was never a problem child. Something didn't seem right, though. Looking at my classmates, I saw several things that didn't align with my life, and I wondered why. Their neatly packed lunches included a sandwich with the crust cut off, green grapes, and a juice box. To me, something as small as individually wrapped items inside sandwich bags meant their families had money. My lunch was free and came on a tray.

My classmate's parents would come in the mornings to read to them in the class. They would chaperone field trips and share their job descriptions during our career days. Their parents would eat lunch with them, often bringing in a McDonald's happy meal. Part of me wished my mom would surprise me with lunch but eating out was a luxury. My classmate's weekends were spent in movie theaters and their summers on family vacations. They had the latest video games, nice shoes, and their clothes always smelled nice. I would later learn that smell was fabric softener. My clothes never smelt like that. A scoop of white powder with pink crystals was used in our house for everything from detergent to bubble bath. I didn't know what real laundry detergent and dryer sheets were until I was old enough to buy them myself.

It's hard to pinpoint when things changed with my mom and my house. I didn't see a subtle shift until the signs of drug addiction were evident and things quickly went from bad to worse.

Sitting in my Godmother's living room, I was frustrated and dreaded the idea of going home. It was a house, but hers was home. Our house was hot, with no electricity, and there was no air conditioner. Going into the refrigerator was forbidden because opening the door would let the last remnants cool out, causing what little food we had to spoil. My house was a place I lived. A roof over my head kept me away from the outside elements, yet somehow other elements always found their way inside. Not the rain or the snow, but the elements of fear, anxiety, instability, and the unknown. At my godmother's house, there were always lights and water. There was always love.

"Ebony, what do you want?" Olivia asked. Looking up at her, fighting tears, I began to say my list.

"I want to get some help for my mom. She needs it. Maybe if I wasn't in the picture, she would have just two mouths to feed instead of three. That could take some of the extra stress off her."

"I want to go to school. I see my friends' parents have these great jobs, and I believe it's because they went to college. I know I need to go eventually, but I don't know how I'm going to pay for it. I could earn a scholarship to play basketball, but that means I need to make the team. Right now, I can't even afford a physical."

"I want to meet a nice guy. Someone who will treat me right, not get drunk and hit my children or me. I want someone who will be there for their kids."

"Is that it?" she asked.

"Yes."

"Well, write it all down and then pray for it."

"Pray?"

"Yes, ask God for what you put on your list."

"But I've never prayed before. How do I do it?" All I've ever prayed was the traditional "Now I lay me" before bed. I heard the deacons at church pray, but my eight-year-old brain didn't feel I was eligible to use the words, "Eternal God our Father."

She said, "Just talk to him like you just did with me."

I was nervous but began to speak. "Dear God, it's me Ebony. I've never prayed before, so I don't know what I'm doing. I have a few things I need." Tears began to roll down my cheeks slowly as I spoke.

"In your name, Amen."

Olivia said, "See, that wasn't so bad, right?" "Now, watch God work."

Fifteen years later, as a senior in college, I began to think about my next moves. Between the applications and job searches, I heard a voice say, "Put God in it." Immediately I was convicted. He had given me everything I'd prayed for sitting in my Godmother's living room.

Right after the Amen, my family moved. I became friends with a young lady who was just as excited to have another girl to play basketball with. Her family sponsored my AAU career, paying for everything from travel expenses to the shoes I played in. When her family got the news of me possibly moving again, they immediately started the process to legally adopt me so I could stay. Her family gave me stability, and that stability afforded me the ability to explore all opportunities. I played basketball and earned a full scholarship to college. I'd also just met a man who had all the qualities I prayed for. He, too, earned an athletic scholarship to play football. His dad cherished his mom, and they're still happily married and active in his life. Everything I wanted.

My Sister Helped Me Heal:

The bible says in Matthew 7:7, "Ask and it will be given, seek and you will find, knock and the door will be opened." And while I received everything I'd prayed for, I still find myself working to figure out how to go to God, especially with the big decisions in my life. The fear I had as an eight-year-old quickly subsides as I remember I can talk to him and he will meet me somewhere between 'now I lay me, and eternal God our father.'

Bio

Ebony Cherry, M.Ed. '22 is an educator and sports coach, serving in Virginia Beach for 16 years. Having a background in Special Education, Ebony advocates for proper outcomes for students diagnosed with a disability and those who teach them. Ebony is also a licensed financial professional whose primary goal is to educate millennials and Gen. "Zers" about the "sandwich generation." Ebony is enthusiastically married to Daryl Cherry, and together they have a nine-year-old daughter, Trinity.

Chapter 5

Uprooting The Seeds

- Tienisha Earl

Growing up, my mother and father fussed, argued, and warred over my twin sister and me. The hatred My mother had towards my father was so great, my sisters and I would be affected by it. My mother would have her favorites; she wouldn't say it, but she would surely show it. My mother would favor some of her daughters more than the others based on how she had felt about our fathers. That caused a great line of division in my sister's and I's relationship. And On the other side, my father would make comparisons with others on how I should do it like someone else because, in reality, he didn't have much faith in me growing up.

So I began to fight inwardly for approval from my mother and father because I just didn't feel like I was enough. Then growing up as a teenager living with my sisters, our relationship was even more toxic. There was no real support for one another. There was no togetherness; we all were divided living under one roof. So I didn't know how to support a sister or how to truly be happy for another woman because I didn't experience much of that growing up.

I began to feel insecure around other women because I would think back to when my ability was compared to another sister of mine or another woman. So I looked at myself very low next to a woman who had more than I, and instead of asking for help or gleaming, I would inwardly envy other women or simply feel intimidated. I would say words like she thinks she is all that or not wanting to give her any compliments or credit. Other times I would shrink back because I didn't think I was good enough to be in the same room with someone that is great. I didn't know what being confident or simply being comfortable in my own skin looked like.

So I would connect to toxic women and call them friends because that is all I've seen. I had a friend who betrayed me in high school by dating a guy I was dating, and I was the type that didn't like confrontation. I didn't even know how to settle conversations without shutting down or fighting. So I avoided it and acted as if it didn't bother me. But it did hurt because that was a close friend of mine. Then years went by as we were all grown up, I was still carrying the pain of the betrayal, along with other things. I built up the confidence to confront the situation, and she lied and said she knew nothing about it. I knew she was lying in my heart, but I avoided confrontation again because I just knew it wouldn't lead to anything good. I wasn't taught to talk it out with my sisters; we either fought or held grudges. In my head, I was shocked we were all grown and she still continued to lie to me. I just couldn't believe that. I only wanted an apology, and I would have forgiven her and let it go.

So with betrayal in my heart, it traveled with me to all of my relationships. So every intimate relationship I got into, I would feel very insecure because I already had it in the back of my head that I wouldn't be good enough because of what was planted in me as a young girl. So I made a promise to myself in my hurt.

Years later when I got married, my husband had to deal with me not trusting him, believing he would cheat on me with other females. I was simply projecting my insecurities on him. I would be at church, and he would shake or hug certain females, and all I saw was betrayal from when I was in high school and insecurities from when I was a young girl. I literally almost tore my marriage apart with assumptions and insecurities. I was begging God to take this pain away. It was hurting my marriage and ministry because I'm called to serve women, and how can I do that holding on to hurt. While I was in bitterness, I would have a closed heart for helping other women out. I wouldn't give the support I knew I could give because of the hurt I endured.

Then one day, after arguing with my husband about another woman who had nothing to do with us, God gave me a revelation that if I didn't get healed, I could lose my marriage. So I started petitioning heaven, asking God to take this bitterness from me because it was really starting to get out of hand, and the unforgiveness I was carrying was going to ruin everything I was connected to.

One evening at my church at a Spring Revival, we had to go to the altar and collect our anointed oils that got prayed over, and my first lady came to me and said to me, "The Lord said that extra bottle of oil you have in your purse, give it to this young lady and without hesitating." I was moved by an open heart and said she has a family-like I do, and I don't know what she might be going through; I just want to love again. When I gave my bottle of anointing oil to that young lady, I was freed from the bondage of betrayal because I decided to believe God and be moved by love. Perfect love casteth out fear. Relying on the love of God cure my hurt. As long as I was holding on to unforgiveness, it kept me from loving the way I was supposed to be loving, but I made up my mind and heart that I would take this journey to get healed, whole, and cleansed. Just because it was planted in me as a young girl doesn't mean I have to live with it; it was time to uproot the seeds planted in me.

Bio

Tienisha J. Earl is a wife to an amazing man of God and a mother to an awesome 11-year-old boy. She loves spending time with her family and friends, but most of all, she loves to push her family and friends to their best. She gets joy in edifying people.

She is a Speaker, Intercessor, Prophetic Voice in the Kingdom, Singer, Prophetic Book Writer, Influencer, Christian Counselor Coach, and Christian Mental Health Specialist Coach.

Tienisha J. Earl struggled with fear and depression for a period of her life and overcame that by the blood of Jesus. She desires to help women overcome fear and depression. Her previous show called "Push Your Purpose" was influenced by her testimony of struggling to live in a low place but still believing and pushing her purpose despite the circumstances. Tienisha J. Earl's motto is, "It's not where you come from, it's who you belong to that determines your destination."

Chapter 6

Sisterhood Helped Me Heal

- Domonique Peele

As I often reflect on my life and how I have blossomed and evolved, I often ask myself how I got from that point (Point A) to this point (Point B)? How did I go from being a woman with rejection and abandonment issues, struggling with insecurity, fear, past traumas, loneliness, brokenness, unforgiveness, depression, and self-sabotaging habits (if we're being honest) to becoming a woman who is thriving in her sisterhood connections, healed, whole, and bold, walking more confidently in my identity and purpose partnering with other women to carry out Kingdom agenda and making hell nervous? We, as women, are a force together. I'm so thankful that although in seasons of my life I may have experienced some hurt and pain in sisterhood and other times I allowed the internal war within take precedence and cause me to run from some relationships that could've potentially been deep-rooted, that during it all I truly learned the art of forgiveness, reconciliation, and restoration. I had to forgive myself and others, release who God wanted me to release, and reconcile with who He wanted me to reconcile with. God is truly the God who allows no pain to go in vain and no void to go unfulfilled. God gave me a second chance and truly allowed the very thing that could've caused me pain to be the thing that caused me to step full force into purpose. I spent many years of my life in isolation because the cave was a safe place for me. I didn't have to let my guard down, be vulnerable, transparent, or open. I didn't have to let anyone in on my mess; at least, I thought this was my safe place, but it was the place the enemy was fighting me the most. I prayed and cried countless nights for God to send me people to connect with.

In 2019, I received a prophetic word that God was about to open a door for me, and many other doors would open through this one door. When I think of God opening doors and manifesting things on the earth, He often does so through people and relationships. I watched this word and truth unfold in my life shortly after. God allowed me to begin to get connected with a tribe of women that helped me walk through a season of deliverance, healing, restoration, and reconciliation. It's true that I, like many others who have dealt with the sting of rejection and abandonment, feared closeness and relationships, so I didn't feel that sisterhood was for me. I felt that I was too broken to be handled and honestly didn't trust that I'd be handled with care but rather dropped, let down, and disappointed, so instead, I'd rather run. God helped me debunk this myth and come out of agreement with words curses I had spoken over my life concerning relationships and obviously didn't allow me to retreat and run from what He was trying to do in this season of my life. I discovered that sisterhood relationships are safe havens where healing takes place through tears, laughter, joy, conversation, prayer, affirmation, empowerment, and gathering. Being surrounded by sisters helps you take off the cape and frees you from the mentality that you have to be perfect and have it all together. It allows you to have a space to be vulnerable, to let your guard down, to let people in who will cover you, correct you, intercede for you and with you, encourage you, hold you accountable, affirm you, and love the pain out of the old wounds. Sisterhood helped me heal, and I no longer had to walk in guilt, shame, condemnation, isolation, and confusion. I'm now bold and courageous. I found my voice, became secure and confident in my identity in Christ, and discovered my purpose, which I believe is to help other women.

I truly pray for the woman reading this now who is still questioning if sisterhood is for her. And to confirm your answer, Yes, sisterhood is for you. I pray that God brings healing to the broken parts of you that have experienced hurt. I pray that He mends the parts of your heart that have been bled on, hurt, and scarred. I pray that the strength of God will overtake you and cause you to be able to forgive yourself and those who hurt, scorned, mocked, ridiculed, shamed, and talked about you. I pray that today as you read this, you come out of agreement with the curse words you've spoken over yourself concerning relationships, partnerships, and divine connections that you don't miss any opportunities and doors that God is opening for you nor the people He is sending your way that will aid in your healing process. Begin to believe again that God has heard your prayers regarding sisterhood and that He cares about every need, including your need for true, genuine, sisterhood connections and that He will answer and send your Mary's and Elizabeth's who will make your baby leap again just like in Luke 1. I pray that you'll experience authentic, genuine, loving sisterhood that will make up for every wound you've experienced in your life. I speak healing to your heart and mind and pray that your confessions and belief will begin to align again and trust that God will allow you to experience healing through sisterhood.

Lastly, I prophesy that same grace to you that God will open one door for you through divine connections with sisters that will change the trajectory of your life and usher you into purpose and destiny and as you brace yourself and navigate through life's journey and all its transitions whether in marriage, ministry, singlehood, motherhood, infertility, career, business, loss, grief, divorce, relocation or even the celebratory moments and seasons of elevation that you'll know that you never have to do life alone.

Bio

Domonique Peele is a native of Portsmouth, Virginia. She obtained her bachelor's of psychology from Chowan University in 2016. She is a mental health counselor, mentor, author, speaker, transformation coach, and all-around change agent. She is the founder of Unleash Her, a God-given idea for a women's group to build community and sisterhood and help women all over be faith-filled, fashionable, fearless, and free. Through her own journey of healing, deliverance, and freedom, she found her voice, identity, purpose, and the beauty for the ashes she endured. Domonique believes it is her God-given assignment to now help unlock cages of women she encounters who too are bound, muzzled, lost, or broken as she once was so that they may be unleashed into the earth. She believes that freedom creates a ripple effect; we're unleashed to help unleash others.

Chapter 7

Candy Jar Sister Testimony

- Lady Candace L. Green

Where do I start? I hope that it's ok to be who I am. I have not had much success in trying to dance to the beat of anyone else's drum other than mine. So, I will stick to my authentic self. I went down the aisles of my life to determine "which" testimony to share. God has just been so many different things for me; my challenge is picking one. All of them hold incredible value, as well as major pivots that happened because of the test, turned testimony. The one that sticks out the most is where I am presently. It is incomplete, but I believe that some testimonies mature over time.

So here we go. Anyone that lives in VA or is close to VA will know exactly where I am headed. I am days away from my husband's one-year anniversary of the Lord deciding to take him home (this is where I take

Candy Jar Sister Testimony

a deep breath and blow it out!) The energy and courage it has taken to make that statement is draining; however, I continue to speak reality, and this is the first testimony of my story; that God has given me the grace and fortitude to say things like that and not fall completely apart (anymore, that is). I would have never thought that now in life, where honey and I were both walking in God's beautiful plan and purpose, that the direction would take a hard left and leave only two footprints on the "purposed" pathway. My thought was, "God, you have got to be kidding. You can go ahead and wake me up now like this is not funny even more." Well, I awakened all right, only to find out I was never dreaming. My entire life shattered into pieces so tiny that many of them were just charrs of glass. Oh, I had big plans for my husband, family, church, and our Marry Me Ministry, all laid out nice, pretty, and organized. There was no stopping the Green team! I missed the memo that God has the last say in plans and not those plans we created in our minds that we thought God would just agree to, especially those that he never authored. I have flipped this situation every way that I could have flipped it to make some type of sense but to no avail. I have been mad, frustrated, angry, confused, irritated, hurt, sad, and any other description that would speak to loss.

I have stayed in that place often, but weirdly enough was still able to handle life, my son, and my church. As mad as I have been with God, I would still get up and thank him that I could still feel the sun on my face, and I could still kiss my son goodbye and pray for safety over him before he left for school. So, the very same God that I asked why for four months and could not talk to him for two of those months is the same God that I still worship and trust through this horrible season of life. My ability to deduce what really was or is happening has been hugely challenging. God has shown me things about myself and brought out areas of opportunity for my life that I would have never seen before my husband's death. One of the many reasons I believe I have been able to live through so many of the most critical moments of this season is because of the many women that stood in the gap for me.

My Sister Helped Me Heal:

I have had support from many different women. There are those that send me daily messages full of life and love. I have had sisters send prayers and scriptures to read when I could not. I have had sisters and daughters cook, clean, play games, go shopping, take trips with, sit, and listen to me, send videos, flowers, books, and any other encouraging things that they could find to just lift my spirits. Honestly, in all transparency, I have been shocked at the amount of support that is continuously received. I have even received testimonies that were shared with me of how women have overcome their own personal obstacles that, at times, have blessed me tremendously. God continues to show His love for me through his children repeatedly. Any time I get to where I feel like I will be stuck in this place for the rest of my life, God arises in one way or another to remind me that He is with me and will never forsake me. My sisters have shown me that they are true women of God and riders that are with me for the long haul. I must say I have in the past had doubts that I would have this type of support, but God is showing me that He has some real agents out here that He sends to heal the broken and destroy the yoke of Satan that would keep His people in bondage. Many times, I felt abandoned and left out here to figure this all out on my own. That idea was immensely irradicated when God gave me Phil 1:6, "Being confident of this very thing, that He who has begun a good work in you will complete it until the day of Jesus Christ." I realized that the word of God and the people of God have surrounded me in a way that covers both my son and me. God will allow things to happen, but He never leaves us out there to die. He is waiting for us to trust Him and His plan for our lives. Trust me, this does not at all scratch the surface of this journey, but I am grateful that thus far, I am still here, and it is by the grace of God.

Bio

Candace L. Green, First Lady of Rock Center Church. Born July 19, 1968, in Hampton, Virginia, Candace L. Green became the fourth daughter of Mr. and Mrs. Melvin & Mary Melton. She is an Alumnus of Hampton High School class of 1986. She attended Commonwealth Community College Business Administration and Thomas Nelson Community College with studies in Early Childhood Development. With her education, she moved on to teach Early Childcare for eight years with NASA Child Development, venturing on to become a Troubleshooting Specialist at Canon for five years. She has proudly earned a Bachelor of Science degree in Psychology at the University of Phoenix. She is currently attending Grand Canyon University in hopes of receiving her Master's in Professional Counseling with an emphasis in Marriage and Family Therapy. One of the happiest days of her life came on October 23, 1999, when she married her lifelong sweetheart Michael D. Green. They have an amazing son Michael D. Green Jr., who they refer to as their miracle son to this union. This life-changing event would catapult her into the wonderful flower we have before us today, none other than Lady Candace L. Green. Under the leadership of her husband, Pastor Michael D. Green, she currently serves as the Founder and Director of Kingdom Beauties for Rock Center Church in Chesapeake, Virginia, Pastoral Intercessor, Praise and Worship team member, Assistant Minister of Music, and a licensed Evangelist Missionary. She also partners with her husband in their "Marry Me" live weekly to empower married couples to live and grow together. Recently, she has launched her personal ministry, "Candy Jar," where she mentors women who feel there is no hope for them and have found themselves in a place of despair. In the illustrious words of Lady Candace Green, "I Will Not Be Silent Any More" (Psalms 107, "let the redeemed of the Lord say so…").

Chapter 8

My Sister Helped Me Heal

- Dr. Charlene Winley

My message is to TRANSFORM, INSPIRE, IMPACT, and EMPOWER women to LIVE a victorious life and triumph over their past traumas and PAIN. I am a woman who has overcome divorce, sexual abuse, homelessness, death of parents and seven siblings, but thank God for taking me through the healing process. I am grateful for the many sisters who lent a listening ear, a shoulder to cry on, a place to stay, and encouraging words throughout various points in my journey. For this book, I will share three specific sisters who gave me language for my trauma and helped me heal through my pain.

I paid the price to stand where I am today. It's a miracle that I am in my right mind, that I am still alive. How can you when your soul was invaded as a child to satisfy lustful needs? It took years for me to

RECOVER myself and be the woman God called and purposed me to be. I know I am POWERFUL, CALLED, and PURPOSED to empower other women to come out of their dark places and walk into their divine purpose.

In the space of four years, my dad, two brothers, grandmother, and mom passed away. My father died one week before I graduated from high school, and my mom passed away three weeks after I graduated from college. During my first year in college, my brother, Derrick, committed suicide. During the second year of college, my brother, Michael, was murdered by his roommate, and we did not find out until four months later. My maternal grandmother died in my junior year of college, and the entire senior year, my mother was terminally ill with breast cancer. The death of my siblings continued as my brother, Paul, died in 1989, my sister Jean died in 2004 while walking across 59th Street in New York City. Ronald, the second born and my oldest brother, died in March 2015. My brother Jesse died of cancer in 2018, and my sister, Audrey, passed away last year in 2021.

Three years after my mother's death, I got married in 1987 and birthed three sons. It was not until the pressure of marriage, motherhood, and financial stress took its toll that I began to realize that something in my life was wrong, incongruous, and did not gel. I experienced a traumatic event at work one day, which caused violent feelings and emotions to surface. I ran inside my classroom, frozen with fear and began crying in the closet. Later that afternoon, I found myself in my therapist's office, Barbara Powell, the first of my sister healer. It was there that I found out in my 30s that I was sexually molested and abused as a child beginning at the age of three. Of course, I did not believe her because I could not have any memory of this. I am a psychology major. She explained that the event occurred when I was pre-language; I didn't have a language for what happened to me and couldn't discuss it or tell anyone.

I relocated to Virginia in 1999 with my three sons, nine, six, and one year old. My head was whirling from all my trauma and now a pending separation and divorce. Virginia thus became my wilderness and the passageway to the promised land. It was here in Virginia that I came face to face with myself. Who I was, what I believed, how did I get here, and how will I turn my life around? True to form, my life continued to unravel in Virginia. Within a year of my relocation, I was served divorce papers and an eviction notice within the same week and thought that this was a sign that I was to move back to New York City. My older brother, a bishop in NYC, told me that if I came back, I would never know what God could do. I did not want to hear this. I did not want to go through the process. I did not want to hurt or suffer, but I knew he was correct. I continued my healing and met my next sister healer, Mary Gay. She walked me through the process of being evicted, separated, and moving into a shelter with my sons. The pain of the divorce was unbearable. It wasn't anything my husband and I discussed. It was his decision, and my attorney informed me that I could stop him from divorcing me.

I realized I jacked up my life and didn't see any value in it. I was a bishop's daughter, and I committed the ultimate sins, adultery and divorce. There was no way out and no way to fix it but end my life. I cried out to God and told him that if He could do anything with my life, He could have it.

I continued processing through my pain while I raised my sons. All seemed to be going well. I was an active member of my church, serving in the ministry and on the praise and worship team. Unbeknownst to me, I was about to face my past. That area of brokenness reared its ugly head and revealed that I still needed more healing. My third sister healer, Dr. LaConda Fanning arrived on the scene and walked me to recovering my broken pieces. She was a prophetic therapist, and she called forth the memories so I could experience healing. She prophesied that I would share my story, author books, and speak healing to other women. I told her I was not going to tell anyone about what I'd been through. All I wanted was to be healed and make the pain go away. Through my experiences, I help women overcome trauma, come out of hiding, and recover their identity to be activated into their purpose and live their life by design and not by default.

Bio

Dr. Charlene D. Winley is a certified life coach, speaker, author, CEO, and founder of ReScriptedLife Coaching and ReScriptedLife Academy. Through her own experiences of sexual and mental abuse, homelessness, divorce, rejection, and grief, Dr. Winley equips women who are struggling with issues regarding Adverse Childhood Experiences, to come out of hiding and recover their identity so that they can live their life on purpose. Dr. Winley has a master's degree in Human Development, Cognition, and Learning from Columbia University with a concentration in Clinical Psychology. She holds a doctoral degree in Educational Leadership from Nova Southeastern University in Florida. She is the vice president of the Attachment & Trauma Network, and a driving force to promote healing of children impacted by trauma through supporting their families, schools, and communities. She is the former 2nd Vice President of the Virginia Beach Branch of the National Association of the Advancement of Colored People, NAACP, Chair of the Education and ACTSO Committee. Dr. Winley, is a best-selling author and published "ReScriptedLife-31 Days to Reconnect with Your Purpose," and co-author of three anthologies; SurvivingHer Anthology-Count it All Joy, God-fident-Stories of Unshakable Faith, and My Sister Helped Me Healed."

Chapter 9

My Plan Didn't Work

- Jessica Simmons

The raindrops created a syncopated rhythm as they hit the window seal to my bedroom. I positioned myself in the fetal position in the middle of my bed with a tear-stained pillow and heavy heart. The weight of the miscarriage, unsteady employment, co-parenting struggles, a new marriage, and raging episodes of depression had convinced me that ending it was better than enduring it. I was a hot mess, broken, angry, and blind. I allowed an invisible veil to cover my eyes for years after leaving my ex-husband. If I did not see it, well, it did not exist. I forced myself into a reality that I could camouflage with the world and that no one, not even the people closest to me, would notice my detachment from life. The pills were there, the intent to end it was there, and I was all alone to carry out what I assumed to be the best solution to my pain. I remember drifting off to sleep after taking half a bottle of Ativan pills and hearing the rhythm once again of the raindrops... splat...drip...splat...drip...splat.

I don't remember much about anything after falling asleep except the blaring sound of my neighbor's horn alerting her daughter to come outside. I instantly became angry because my plan failed. I was still living. I was still in the fight of my life that I was battling silently. No one knew of my struggle, my pain, or my despair. I hid it very well! I still showed up to lead worship on Sundays, attended family functions and events, and was still attentive and present for my husband and son but dying on the inside. I lived in the shadows of my hurt and trauma for years. Understand this however, my life was not always bad. It was a handful of uneventful, hurtful, shameful, and disrespectful events that corrupted my mind from being at peace.

For some reason, I took on the weight of what others did to me and the occurrences that pierced my soul instead of releasing the hurt in the proper places. When I got up, I checked my phone, and I had a message from a woman who was acquainted with my husband who said she wanted to talk with me and give me what God told her to speak over me. I was so hesitant because I had never had any real conversation with her, and there was no way I would allow my private battle to become public. My trauma was literally taking over my life, and I knew I needed an escape but didn't know how to get there. Trauma is like a gaping hole that sucks you in piece by piece. It starts with your mind and then your heart and works its way down until you are completely consumed in it. No matter how much you try to pull back, something like the breeze of a fall day will remind you of the way your face was in pain after another fight and fresh bruises, seeing a mother and baby in the checkout line in Walmart after another failed month of trying to conceive or feeling alone in a room full of people. Trauma isn't an inviting door, but it's more like a long road with many loops, bends, and bridges, but no real exit. That day, I begged God to pull me out of my own darkness!

My Sister Helped Me Heal:

I was so tired of masking the hurt and shame that I finally decided to advocate for myself and reach back out; honestly, I had nothing to lose. I went to church and met with her in a private room, and she even had another woman of God come in the room to talk with me and pray. Their prayer was sincere, and I connected with every word they uttered unto God. That day, I felt the chains and weight of all my failures, hurt, embarrassment, and abandonment loose their hold on me, and I was able to breathe. Breathe without my chest tightening! Breathe without any form of worry! Breathe with the intention to face my issues head-on! I COULD BREATHE! Those women (now major contributors to my village) saved me from me!

Because of their prayers and support, I was able to finally locate a therapist and talk through my pain. I was able to address some hurt that I had buried so well, and I was finally brave enough to tell the enemy that everything he fed me for years was a lie. The beautiful part of my story is that the women who prayed for me and took time to minister to me had no idea that just a day or two before, I attempted suicide. They were obedient to God and reached out even though they did not know the full story. Honestly, many of the women of my church had no idea of the battle that I was in, but through their love, smiles, hugs, random text messages, and continuous support, they helped me heal.

I was able to heal because I had women in my path who understood the assignment that a simple check-in could change the trajectory of a person having a bad day, but in my case, it helped to stop the plan of ending their life. Having supportive sisters allowed me to heal from physical abuse, low self-esteem, emotional abuse, and mental illness. The deeply layered trauma began to fall when I experienced true sisterhood! I learned the effectiveness of communication and transparency. I learned the vitality of fellowship and intercession, but most of all, I learned the importance of heeding to the voice of God.

I am so glad my plan did not work! Now, I enjoy the rain and the rhythm that I heard that day because I have seed in the ground, and all the weight of my trauma has fallen off, and I am now reaping a bountiful harvest!

Bio

Minister Jessica D. Simmons is the youngest daughter of Della Hall. A native of Norfolk, Virginia. Jessica received her education in the Norfolk Public School system, where she earned her advanced diploma from Norview High School in 2005. Upon completing high school, she furthered her education at Tidewater Tech and graduated from the Practical Nursing program in 2007. She served as a Licensed Practical Nurse, offering her medical expertise and knowledge for over ten years. In 2018, Jessica ventured into the field of Human Services and Social work and currently serves as the Program Manager for Team Up Mentoring. Jessica launched her business, Beautiful Blossoms Christian Coaching LLC, in 2018, where her mission is to help women heal healthy and whole. She is married to her devoted husband, Kevin, and they share two children, Cameron and Aubriegh-Rae. Jessica is an example of perseverance and believes that we can grow wherever we are planted.

CHAPTER 10

A Divine Meet-up

- Pastor Paulette Harper

*E*veryone experiences a hard time in life, but no one really knows its detrimental effects on a person's emotional or spiritual well-being.

I had no idea that those hard times would include coming face to face with emotional trauma, nor could I even imagine what those greatest moments in my life would look like.

How could I find the strength to come back after a 23-year marriage ended?

How many of you have experienced a major disruption in your life that you had no idea how you were going to make it?

I was going through one of the darkest moments in my life. Yet, I knew that God was with me, and He would not only walk with me but carry me every step of the way.

A Divine Meet-up

I was broken, scared, and empty except for the gamut of emotions I was now experiencing, from hopelessness, severe depression, feelings of fear, loneliness, shame, and even thoughts of suicide.

For four years, God hid me from those in our church and those who watched the emotional trauma almost kill me. Our divorce was messy, yet, God continued putting me on the potter's wheel to bring me to a place of deliverance. There was some deep work He needed to do before He'd allow me to face friends and foes.

I was isolated except for my family. They gave me moral support but not spiritual support, and that's what I needed.

Even in the darkest moments of life, God was there all the time. He gave me glimpses of hope when, out of nowhere, two sisters from the past crossed my path. One was a phone call from another pastor's wife, whom I hadn't seen or heard from in years. The moment I heard her voice—the water dam broke. The tears gushed down my face in relief because she was exactly who I needed at that moment. As a former pastor's wife, I didn't have many friends I could confide in, but God knew I needed someone I could trust and build a solid sister girl relationship with. And he brought her back into my life for those very reasons.

She knew we were going through a divorce, so I didn't have to fill her in all the details. We talked daily on the phone and met weekly in a park for prayer. We not only studied the word, but she brought me the book Purpose Driven Life by Rick Warren, which was part of our regiment.

From that moment forward, I was on my way to complete healing, spirit, soul, and body.

For years, she watched me go through my own metamorphosis. The transformation of rebuilding my life again — without the man I had grown to love but with the King of Kings who loved me enough to send a life jacket my way. Today she and I are the best of friends. I couldn't have asked God to bring anyone else. She listened to the Holy Spirit and made that call.

I remember bumping into a gentleman in the women's restroom at a church we were visiting. You talk about time and province meetings. Only God could do something like that!

My Sister Helped Me Heal:

We hadn't seen each other in years either. Our children went to the same preschool and had the same babysitter when they were kids, but when life sent us in different directions, he and I lost contact.

When we had that God encounter in the bathroom, I was facing my life transition of going through my divorce, and she was dealing with life as well.

We hugged and exchanged numbers, and that was almost twenty years ago.

We bonded immediately over lunch and phone calls, just listening to each other tell our stories of how life changed both of us. We shared stories about our children, but most of our time was developing our bond of what real sisterhood meant.

We learned to confide in each other and build a solid relationship on trust, God, and a genuine need to connect. We could share our deepest secrets with each other knowing that neither one of us would break the code of silence.

We've grown to know each other's pet peeves, likes, and dislikes. She knows I'll walk out of a movie if the movie is going in the wrong direction, and I know her all too well that she'll go and ask for a refund for the same movie. The laughs we share have been built on spending quality time together.

We both are Christians, and we've built our friendship on our love for Christ and His word. Our Sunday mornings are shared with text messages about something Bishop Jakes has preached or something the Lord has revealed.

Our friendship also extends to the prayer closet. We have prayed for each other while we've faced our own disappointments and heartaches. And have celebrated our successes and victories.

When we're out in public, people think we are real sisters because we look alike, believe it or not. When they ask, "Are you sisters?" We've learned over the years to just say, "Yes."

I'm blessed to have her be part of my journey. She's shown me just how essential our friendship is and what it really means to have a sister for life.

Time and divine intervention had kissed, and it was in those moments I knew His hand was still on my life, and He indeed had more for me to do.

These two sisters took me under their wings, prayed for me, spoke the Word over my life, and helped me to see there was another chapter in my life to write.

> *"I'll show up and take care of you as I promised and bring you back home. I know what I'm doing. I have it all planned out— plans to take care of you, not abandon you, plans to give you the future you hope for.*
>
> *(JEREMIAH 29:11 MSG)*

Bio

Paulette Harper is a twelve-time # 1 Amazon bestselling author, certified story coach, business coach, five-figure anthology expert, and the CEO of Elevate Her Story University: Coaching Academy.

Paulette uses her gifts to equip ambitious Christian women speakers and entrepreneurs to write, publish books, and be the catalyst for transformation in their spheres of influence. She is committed to empowering women and equipping them with tools to unapologetically share their voices and stories, as well as helping them push past barriers and discover their purpose so that they may become the best version of themselves.

As a minister of the Gospel, she has devoted her life to sharing the message of hope on as many platforms as possible. Paulette preaches, "Live with purpose. Don't limit God. Stay focused and allow God to take you places you have only imagined."

Connect with Paulette Website www.pauletteharper.com

Section 2

Chapter 11

I am a Woman of Life

- Lakia Perez

In this chapter, you will see how the ministry that God birthed through me helped me heal through loss, grief, and pain. When pursuing purpose, we never consider that our purpose is not just for us to serve others, but God allows us to be the first partakers of the blessing that flows from it. God created us for a purpose. Ephesians 2:10 says, "For we are his workmanship, created in Christ Jesus for good works, which God prepared beforehand, that we should walk in them." Here is my Story!

In 2010, while on military assignment in California, the Lord dealt with me about the women's ministry. He gave me the name Women of Life. I prayed and asked God for guidance on how to move forward. He revealed the women that would serve with me. I reached out to them and asked them to come to California. When they came, I shared what

God said, and they agreed, and that's when Women of Life was birthed. The mission is to encourage, empower, uplift, and unite women, and we did this through the ministry of Prayer.

In January 2011, I reported to my new duty assignment in Virginia. Although my military assignment changed, my spiritual assignment was still moving forward and growing. During this time, my sisters, Devonna, Mia, Tasha, and I grew the ministry. We were consistent in having morning prayer at 6:00 am and bringing forth encouraging words to the ladies daily. It was a blessing how God orchestrated this connection and how this ministry fulfilled all our purposes. Only God can do something like this!

In June 2011, I received a call from a family member stating that my mother's kidneys shut down and I had to come quickly. When I arrived, my mother was septic and was in the ICU. I traveled back and forth from Virginia to New Jersey every weekend to be with my mom. This was very taxing mentally, emotionally, physically, and financially. Eventually, I was able to get a hardship transfer from the military to be with her more often. This was not easy. I had to leave my two sons with a friend while I cared for my mom. Every day was a faith day. I thank God for my sisters for keeping me lifted during those trying times.

My mother had to undergo several surgeries and had many bad prognoses. However, we continued to pray and believed God for a mighty move in her life. As a praying woman, I just knew that God would hear my prayer, heal my mom, and raise her from that hospital bed. I was confident because it was not just me praying but also Women of Life and a host of family and friends. I felt the strength of God, especially when the girls came to New Jersey to be with me and prayed and anointed my mom. One day she got up and was getting stronger. I was so excited. My mom talked about bringing her family to Christ after she got out of the hospital. We began to see hope. As my mother was getting better, my dad started to get ill. My dad was dealing with several illnesses but was taking diligent care of himself. I did not know that he was as sick as he was. He was hospitalized. Now I had two parents in the hospital. I was running from one hospital to the next in opposite cities. I did not understand why this was happening to me. I kept saying, "God, this is too much for me to manage."

My mom's health took a bad turn, and she needed surgery. So, as we prepared for her surgery, my mom said to me, "Kia, go be with your dad and just come back and pray with me before my surgery in the morning." My dad passed away that evening, and I stayed there until his body was picked up. I was so broken-hearted, but I knew I had to be there with my mom. The next morning, I went to my mom, prayed with her, and told her what happened, but I remained strong. That was the last time I saw my mom awake. Two weeks later, she passed away, and two weeks after that, my grandfather passed. You can imagine how broken I was. I became depressed, isolated, shut down, and consumed with grief. It was hard for me to pray, let alone encourage someone else with all this loss. I was not thinking about ministry.

However, the ladies were still there praying, encouraging me, and lifting me up. The grief and loss that I experienced felt like it would consume my whole life, and I would not be able to shake it. I thank God for my sisters Devonna, Mia, Tasha, and The Women of Life ministry for pouring into me and reminding me that there is still Life after death. As I look back now, all I can say is, "If I had not said yes to God and birth the ministry, how and where would I be today? See, God knows all things, and He knows exactly what we need. During my time of despair, He poured back into me through the women of God and reminded me that I am a Woman of Life. I want to encourage you and tell you that life may throw many blows, and you may be one who experienced loss and grief like I did, but do not drop your baby (purpose/ministry). It will be the very thing that will breathe life back into you. I want to leave you with this scripture, Psalm 34:18. The LORD is close to the brokenhearted and saves those who are crushed in spirit. I can honestly say that He did that for me and continues to do it. Remember that you are a Woman of Life!

Bio

Lakia Perez is a woman after God's heart with a passion for ministry. She is the mother of two awesome young men, Noel and Donaven. A Retired twenty-year Veteran of the United States Navy. She received her BA in Psychology at Saint Leo's University in 2017. A co-author in the anthology "Residue of War." She is a spiritual mother to many and strives to impart life-giving encouragement and comfort through teaching and preaching the word of God. She oversees Women of Life Ministries and is the Executive Director of The Christian Life Radio Station located in Norfolk, Virginia. Serving as a conduit of God's healing, she has been privileged to witness the miraculous and transformative power of God's love in her life and in the life of many she has touched.

CHAPTER 12

Darkness didn't Stop my Healing

- Ronjeanna Unorthodox
Certified Wellness Coach

I wonder if the ten-year-old or fifteen-year-old me thought this day would ever be experienced. I had countless moments during my life when amazing women assisted me in my journey of what I felt at that time was unbearable. I, for years, battled with identity and the acceptance of who God created me to be. This battle led to decisions that created mental setbacks. Life circumstances also played a huge role in the process. I personally had the mindset that my calling was the purpose of taking me out as a kid, along with that, suffering from depression and not realizing it then. My mother was in and out of the mental hospital during most of my youth, and I was terrified. My mother back then suffered from PTSD, Chemical imbalance, and depression. An amazing, powerful, chosen vessel of God, she was a major threat to hell's kingdom back then, and the enemy wanted to take her out. So, of course, I was like, keep that calling, I didn't want any parts. God started dealing with me at a young age in the gift of seeing prophetically, and I fought it to the max. So, to drown it out along with life, I started picking up hindering habits and ways to blind my focus.

The experiences were often induced choices. I became a mother at sixteen years old, miscarried a second child, and birthed the third child at nineteen years old. The father of my first born was not who God had selected for me. When the relationship didn't work the way I fantasized, I became devasted and depressed. Now sixteen-year-old, I was still a kid, to be honest. (This began the unhealthy cycles of relationships.) My mother, even in her battles, was right there to push me and speak life to me. There were women organizations in my community that made sure teen moms continued education and graduated. I was covered when I didn't realize it. The sisters in the church community helped me in those moments when I was weak. Moving forward into my adulthood, mind you, I was still stacking bad habits. Now don't get me wrong, I also had great accomplishments. After several failed relationship attempts, my assigned King found me. We eventually got married. Things were great and challenging. Sounds weird, right? But it's the truth. I grew up mainly in a Baptist Church. For a short period, my family did attend a Pentecostal ministry for a little while during my childhood. I had never really healed from certain experiences I saw at such a young age. Getting back to moving into adulthood, married now.

Now living in a different area (Hampton Roads). I was raised on the eastern shore of VA. So I was established in the seven cities working in the medical field. I eventually found a church to join. Different flow non-denomination. I first received the holy ghost evidence speaking in heavenly languages. I stayed there for a while, then left and joined another ministry. I learned a lot and was growing but still very immature spiritually. This timeline of events was 2003-2006. Things were going well, but there were those lingering insecurities, hurts, doubts, and anger I was secretly battling from my past mentally. I had a husband and a mother of two at the time. I then faced a bump in my marriage. Listen, that was a moment that I was literally feeling defeated. I questioned everything on a mega, unhealthy level.

During my journey, I met a beautiful soul through the indie music industry that became my big sis spiritually and naturally. Karen Stockard helps me through such a dark moment. She spoke life to me and my circumstance. Things were looking shaky. I don't know how I would have gotten through without her in my life during that time. God saved my marriage in 2007. I decided to move forward in my medical field career and become an LPN. Two weeks into the program, I found out I was pregnant; mind you, my youngest daughter was ten years old. Then to top that, my middle daughter's biological father filed for full custody, asking for full rights in 2008. That was the ugliest custody battle ever. I felt like things weren't working in my favor. Lawyers, house inspections, questioning my daughter. The experience horribly impacted her. She was only ten.

The pressure was stacking. Remember, I had not fully dealt with proper healing. It was only small breakthroughs and Band-Aid fixes. It was my mom, Minister Barbara Smith, my sister Regina Smith, and sister Evangelist Karen Stockard again that helped me through that moment. Now God did show his mighty hand, and I got full custody of my daughter. Even in the victory, behind those scenes were a bad habit that I was once released from. Drinking has emerged back in my life. I started building to become my escape. I started getting bad, and I eventually left the ministry I was serving as an ordained evangelist under and went full-fledged back into the streets partying, drinking, acting just wild. I let hurt and issues in ministry (that I had not been trained to deal with at the time) cost me to frown upon the ministry and literally ran. It wasn't until 2012 that I met two ladies that would contribute to my coming out of a deep-running pit that was tunneling.

That journey took years 2012 to 2018, battling and running from my chosen hood and calling. My sister and nursing peer invited me to her church in 2012. I had major reservations. I was not trying to let my guard down ever again. But something was pulling at me to visit. I went and met some amazing women who saw the oil on my life and didn't give up on me. Pastor Rebecca Duckworth never gave up on me. I joined the church in 2012 but was running from my purpose, and I mean hard. Pastor Rebecca Ducksworth never stopped reaching out, checking on me, and speaking life. I eventually surrendered in 2018. I finally gave a real yes. I got delivered from being a severe alcoholic, smoking, and healed from several health conditions that had become life-threatening for me at one point. God had women of powerful purpose in my life journey throughout the years till now that helped me to my rewarding breakthrough. Now I can effectively help others.

My Sister Helped Me Heal:

Bio

Ronjeanna Harris is a God-fearing and chosen ordained Evangelist, affirmed Prophet and Intercessor. Ronjeanna is a wife, mother of six, and grandmother. This game-changer is the proud owner of Just Jeanna's Skin Care LLC. Natural Product creator & Formulator was launched as a company in 2018 after much prayer, research, and preparation. After just two years in business, Just Jeanna's Skin Care LLC got approved to be in the Walmart marketplace in 2020. Ronjeanna is a Published Author, LPN, and award-winning Certified Wellness Coach with over 20 years of experience and skill in the healthcare industry. Just Jeanna's Skin Care LLC offers a host of local, national, and international services. This trailblazer, in May 2021, started her own nonprofit organization, Jeanna's iFeed, doing what she loves, which is being a servant. Kingdom Solutionist coaching & mentoring services was birthed in 2021. Community serving and giving back is an honor and passion for Ronjeanna. Providing natural wellness solutions is Ronjeanna mission to stand by.

www.justjeannas.com

CHAPTER 13

Hidden in insecurity to walking in purpose confidently

- Antoinette Hines

Hidden in plain sight right before their eyes, people overlooked me, and I liked it that way. Comparison made me insecure, and I lacked confidence in what I knew God placed in me. Hearing God since I was very young, I told my grandmother, and she encouraged me to not speak of what I was hearing for fear that I might be misunderstood. Family compared how I sounded, sang, and looked to everyone around me, which fed my insecurity and lack of confidence. Growing up in the church, I have seen the good and ugly of leaders but was able to stay clear. I felt extremely comfortable hiding in the back of the church even as I matured. Avoiding encountering people on the pulpit and altar helped me stay hidden. Leaving home, I joined the United States Army. No matter where the Army sent me, I always prioritized finding a church to faithfully attend. Texas, Georgia, South Korea, Kansas, Iraq, and Belgium across my career, finding a place to worship and be spiritually fed was a must.

Hidden but serving, I so desperately want God's presence with me no matter where I am or was. So much so that I spent more time in the church than I did at home, cleaning, choir practice, dance practice, bible study, and Sunday Services. I was so busy serving that I left my family uncovered of my presence, and I was unbalanced. Leaders love you serving and sowing, but change the flow of money, your time spent, and you become something you are not. My character came under attack. Gladly came my Permanent Change of Station to Kansas, I was trying to find my balance after being hurt by church leadership. I lost my confidence in myself, ministry, and the leaders who claim to love God's people. In Kansas, I met a beautiful soul named Nicole Powell, a Minister, as I later found out. We worked together, and it was on the job that God was restoring my faith in the church. Nicole invited me to her church, and reluctantly, we attended the service. We joined a month later and got to work. She nurtured my hunger for God while addressing some of my hurt from ministry leaders.

God used Nicole to wipe away my church hurt and poured into me as a woman. She helped me reestablish my faith in God, leaders, and myself. She made me look in the mirror at myself. I gained confidence in who God made me to be and strengthened my voice. The transformation was evident in working with 310 young ladies we were responsible for. For some, we were trainers, counselors, motivators, sisters, and friends when helping them take on motherhood in the Army while maintaining and exceeding the Army Physical Fitness standards to get back in the fight. My passion came alive working with these young ladies. We had the unique opportunity to see them blossom into successful Soldiers and mothers. Meeting Nicole was a divine setup by God in my process of gaining my confidence and walking into my purpose.

Time was up in Kansas and on to Belgium. The setup by God is real. He will truly take you to a foreign land to separate and build you in your process. Three weeks in the country, we were led to Word of Truth

International Christian Ministries under Pastor Gavin E. Wainwright Sr. and Lady Angela M. Wainwright. When you walk through the church doors, you feel the overwhelming love of God. The church comes alive and the hunger is fed when Pastor Wainwright preaches and teaches. Lady Wainwright had this extraordinary smile that melted all your reservations away. Her voice was that of an angel here on earth. Every word from her lips was filled with love, even in correction. She had the supernatural ability to meet you right where you were and speak life to your soul. There was no way you could be in her presence and not be lifted or changed. She was a MEGA faith-filled woman after God's heart. Lady Wainwright greeted us with her beautiful smile and quickly said, "I heard you singing, ma'am, you're joining the praise team." She gave me the rehearsal schedule and requirements for the choir and praise team. I stated that I love to dance, and she introduced me to the dance coordinator. Just like that, I knew she meant business! Her motto is, "Whatever you do for God, do it with excellence!" Every time I tried to sit down and hide, Lady Wainwright snapped me back with the word of God.

After a year, my leaders promoted me to Director of the Dance Ministry. Fear came; it was a huge responsibility to be over four praise dance teams. I again compared myself to someone else's shoes in ministry. Pastor and Lady Wainwright encouraged me to focus and keep seeking the Lord to develop as a leader. Weekly, Lady Wainwright, sent emails of encouragement with scripture for our journeys in life. My leaders told me there is no comparison in the body of Christ. We each have a role and part, and we are supposed to be different. That shifted my mindset and renewed my passion for ministry. The anointing flowed as she said it would from the youngest child to the teens and women. God provided the knowledge to teach at each level, and the children were moved by the Holy Spirit in a mighty way. It was amazing to see what God would do using me. My fear became faith. I got to see the power of God move in our youth and see them mature in their knowledge of the word and God's ways. My leaders saw in me what I could not see in myself, and I am forever grateful they trusted the God in me. I started walking into purpose with confidence because of their Godly love, direction, and teachings.

My Sister Helped Me Heal:

Bio

I am Mrs. Antoinette Hines, CEO of Uniquely Me, LLC., wife, mother of six beautiful diamonds, grandmother of two, and a Minister. An Amazon #1 Best selling author, Amazon #1 International Best selling author, and podcaster. As a financial awareness and literacy advisor, I help people assess their financial picture, working to transform the mindset from Poverty to Prosperity. Connecting people to their personal, relational connections with their finances is a passion. Impact, empower, and position, I encourage everyone right where they are to save AND invest while living the good life! Travel, music, and ministry are a must-have for me. I am a worshipper at heart, I love the Lord, and I walk by faith. I look forward to walking on this transformation journey with people who want a better life financially. I am the MIRROR CHECK Queen!

Process your Pain, fulfill your Purpose with Power while Postured and Positioned through Passion; we gain Progress to become Productive!

CHAPTER 14

The Angel that Helped Me Heal

- MICHELLE FRANKLIN

Throughout my life, many people have come along and helped me through my journey. However, there is one particular young lady I like to highlight. Her name is Dr. Frances Anna Bailey. I chose to write about her because she is selfless. I have never had to ask her to pray, encourage me, or just be there. It's like she knows when I need her to encourage me. I've had five surgeries, and I'm preparing for my 6th surgery as I write this chapter. Frances encourages me that I'm needed. As a leader, you need to hear that you are needed and appreciated.

She doesn't ask me for anything, and she's always asking what she can do to assist me. No one knows how hard it is to keep going, especially when you are not being acknowledged for your true value. I'm not just pressing to keep going, but I feel like Sophia from the color purple at times. *"All my life I had to fight."* Most times, I did it alone. I'm a single woman with two kids, and unfortunately, I didn't have the support in life that many others had. I didn't have anyone telling me, hey, you're going to make it or reminding me that I was born to be an overcomer and help others overcome.

When I started my coaching school, I never thought it would become all it has become. It was through my coaching school that I met Frances. Since I met her, I have fought harder. I may cry in private, but each day I quote the words Frances always reminds me of, "You're needed." Frances is just one of many in this season that has helped me. I chose to talk about her because at my weakest moments, times I want to throw in the towel, out of the blue, she texts me and reminds me who I am. God sent an angel to encourage me, and I truly believe it's her. The Bible says in *Hebrew 13:2, Do not forget to show hospitality to strangers, for by so doing some people have shown hospitality to angels without knowing it.* This passage of scripture informs us that sometimes angels come in the form of humans. As you read this book, I want you to ask yourself, who is your angel? How do you know it's your angle? And what have you learned or overcome because of their presence?

Now let's look at encouragement. Encouragement means to inspire with courage in spirit and hope. Encouragement is the key ingredient needed to help pull someone out of the trenches. When you're sick, facing homelessness, grieving, or just struggling with life, it takes encouragement to get you up. The Bible says in *Proverbs 13:12, Hope deferred makes the heart sick, but a longing fulfilled is a tree of life.* That means, when what you're hoping for hasn't come to pass yet, you could find yourself sick. I truly believe sickness hit my body because I suffered in silence with so many questions for years. Why haven't my core promises and prayers fully manifested yet? I'm 42 and still single; 20 years single, to be exact. As a matter of fact, I promised God that I would keep myself pure until my husband came, only if He gave me the strength. I have married friends and family members, yet no one thinks I'm a good fit for their single friends. Then, of course, there's God, Jesus, my Lord and Savior.

Sometimes, I secretly question if He would hold up His end of the bargain. Yeah, as if I should be bargaining with my Creator. Living life alone and raising two children is not how life is supposed to have been, but honestly, it's been great. Challenging, yet peaceful, and drama-free. Nevertheless, when you desire to be loved by someone (intimately), it could definitely make the heart grow sick, which can have a tremendous impact on the body. Am I blaming every sickness I've suffered on singleness? Absolutely not! I'm simply saying, for me, it puts more stress on the parts of me that were weakened. This book is being produced in the latter part of a pandemic. Many of us have had to pull ourselves up and fight to produce in the midst of losing loved ones, jobs, clients, homes, and even those facing divorce. I've lost a total of nine loved ones, struggled with trying to grow my business in a world that says at 42, I should have been a millionaire by now. I've struggled to preach the gospel and navigate through a pandemic while battling sickness in my body. Believe it or not, through all the hits I've taken, mentally, I've been ok.

It's my mind that has kept me. What's the Secret? My foundation and, of course, my angel. Having a foundation rooted in Christ doesn't mean I won't get hit. It means when I do get hit, I'll receive the strength to get back up. I'm here to tell you that sometimes your foundation in Christ isn't enough. Sometimes you need those angles. You need to find yourself a Frances Anna Bailey.

Growing up in church, I was consistently reminded that God uses three things in life to help us. Faith, Family, and Friendship. It's up to you to push back the hurt and feelings of abandonment and connect to your Frances. Allow your Savior to lead you to the people that can help you heal. The person who won't force you to heal quickly but in a healthy manner. The person who doesn't mind being a supporter, rather it's in word or deed. Everyone has their own problems; it's all about creating balance to help and support who you need to help. I'm very knowledgeable, and because I have a desire to see everyone accomplish their purpose, God has connected me to people who push me to keep going. Not for their benefit but for mine and God's.

Bio

Michelle Franklin has had the privilege of being trained by The John Maxwell Team, Dr. John Veal, and Dr. Anthony Tiller of American Christian Chaplaincy.

Michelle Franklin has demonstrated effective organizational and communication skills throughout her 19 years in Ministry and the Marketplace. She has exceptional leadership skills, management skills, and is considered a solution-oriented leader. She's skilled in critical thinking, conflict resolution, and a team player who encourages and influences leaders to mature and flow in one accord. She prides herself in building strong relational and interpersonal skills within teams and believes in professionalism and ministerial ethics to the highest degree.

Some of her experiences include counseling, coaching, speaking, teaching, and training leadership teams. She's a published author of 10 books, and is set to release three more in the coming year!

Michelle Franklin is also a Licensed Notary and Loan Signing Agent in the state of IL, and can accommodate all your notarizations and signing needs.

CHAPTER 15

Covered

- Dr. Charlene Bell

"I would do you and a disservice if I didn't tell you... to come up higher, Charlene!"

Those words rang in my ears like a fire alarm! Come up higher, come up higher, any higher, and I might've loss consciousness from the altitude! Those words caused a pause in my spirit because I've heard them before. What did they mean "come up higher? What was the blueprint? Did they even know what it meant? And if so, why not tell me what "come up higher required?"

As early as I can remember, I've always been "just Charlene," I was the last to develop, the last picked for games, the last picked for dances, the last. So going into adulthood, I made it a point to be the greatest at everything I did. I always wanted to do things "the right way," "look the right way," and I never once wanted to "look like a failure." In my immature mind, I had to be the best for people to love me, so I needed it to be perfect! How would people stay around if I wasn't perfect? I became so critical of myself to the point that when I did make a mistake, I would retreat and isolate myself.

"Growing up not feeling good enough is a heavy burden to bear as a child."

Have you ever felt so alone in the world, like no one understood you? I had this mindset, and for years, it kept me in the dark cave where I dressed it, set up utilities, and made a home in isolation. I found every reason why I wasn't good enough, why I wasn't a good friend, why I wasn't pretty enough, the list went on and on. I finally realized that the issue wasn't necessarily me (some people added to my cave experience). Throughout my life, I've had some amazing women pour into me. Women that prayed with me and for me, cried with me, fought with me, and even preyed on me (but that's for another anthology, lol). It was hard to trust new friendships because there was always a thought in the back of my mind whether they genuinely liked me for me. Let me be clear, I have always been the life of the party. I don't say that arrogantly, but you know there's always that one friend that makes life better, that is me. So, my mere presence was overwhelming for most, and I started to shrink just to fit in.

Can you imagine it? God made me an illuminating light, and because people forgot their shades, they became frustrated with God's brilliance in me. I believe God places people in your life to help uplift you and push you toward your purpose; that's what Sonya McMannen-Taylor did for me. This is my story. Dun, dun, dunnnn (in my Law & Order: SVU voice)!

I remember the first day we met. I was loud, boisterous, possibly obnoxious, and over the top, while Sonya was the total opposite. I'd never met someone like her growing up. She grew up with siblings, both parents in the home, and even homeschooled. To say we were from different sides of the track was an understatement. It seemed we were from different planets, but little did I know that our differences would be what knitted us together.

Sonya walked with a sense of prestige and honor about herself that was downright regal and revered by many. Over the years, our relationship blossomed into a beautiful friendship. We'd travel together, go to concerts and plays together, and just have fun.

For ten years, we served in ministry together. We watched one another blossom in ministry and grow in our callings. But in Jan 2021, the dynamics of our relationship took a pivot.

After serving 12 years in a ministry, my husband of 12 years heard the voice of the Lord tell him it was time to leave and serve in another ministry. What?!! Why didn't God inform me? I mean, I'm an ordained Evangelist. Why bypass me? A Tsunami of thoughts rushed into my mind of where we would be serving and if I would fit in, who would understand me and love me for me.

Change can be scary for someone who dealt with years of rejection. It's almost like being the new kid on the block or even a senior at a new high school. A certain level of respect comes with being an upperclassman, but when you are in a new place, it's like being a freshman all over again.

Have you ever had someone in your life who, no matter what you've done or where you've come from, genuinely wants the best for you? Not just naturally but spiritually? That's Sonya McMannen-Taylor for me.

I remember a time during a praise dance rehearsal and breaking down because I felt so defeated and guilty about my son's autism diagnosis. I remember Sonya stopping rehearsal and instructing all the women to create a circle and dance around me until the heaviness broke off.

I knew from that day that our relationship would forever be connected, and that God put someone in my life that I could trust. In ministry, it's hard to find people who will love you even when you don't love yourself. Someone who will see greatness in you, help develop you, and not use your faults against you. Someone who will be honest with you, correct you when you're wrong, and love you all at the same time. It's a rarity but once found, it's refreshing.

I currently serve at Revelation Church under the divine leadership of Pastor Jason and... you may have guessed it, my friend and leader, Prophet Sonya McMannen-Taylor.

I appreciate her prayers and sensitivity in the spirit. When death was on me, she prayed against it. When depression wrapped me like a warm blanket, she took the time to remove it. Never judgmental or aggressive but gentle, caring, and loving. I see now what it means to be covered!

Bio

Dr. Charlene Bell is a Certified Family Nurse Practitioner, United States Navy Veteran, and founder of Her Padded Truth, a company committed to providing women with safe, cost-effective, and eco-friendly feminine hygiene products. As a healthcare provider, she has extensive knowledge in Adult, Geriatric, Mental Health, and Women's health.

She served as a Navy Corpsman, helping those she served, which led her to her calling as a healthcare provider.

A native of the Bronx, New York, she obtained most of her education while serving overseas in the United States Navy. She obtained her Doctor of Nursing from Frontier Nursing University, Master of Nursing from Walden University, Associates in Nursing from Medical Careers Institute, Masters in Business Administration with a concentration in Health Management from American InterContinental University, and Bachelors in Healthcare Administration from the University of Phoenix. She is an advocate for Women's health and Women's right and is the visionary behind Her Padded Truth, a nonprofit organization serving homeless women in the Hampton Roads area with menstrual hygiene products.

Chapter 16

They (She) helped me find ME!

- Alexis Ganier

"I don't know what else to do," I said, exhausted as I sat in my room feeling so broken, confused, and unsure of my future. I knew I needed to get out of the place I was in. I just didn't know how, I didn't know then, but I know now that it was God pulling me, and it wouldn't allow me to rest. At that time, I found myself drinking every day, looking for some form of comfort. I had finally hit my low place, and God intervened just in time. I was searching for something, but I was looking in all the wrong places. I struggled with what was next for me. I was in a stuck place, and it was going to take something much greater than me to get me out of the position and posture that I was in. I couldn't breathe anymore because I wasn't living; I was existing. Life; I no longer had the joy, happiness, peace, and love that God wanted me to have. I was literally going through the motions of life, waiting on another person/thing to dictate my next. I wasn't in control of myself because I lived in my emotions, and I had no sense of direction for life.

I was in a dark place! Walking around depressed, barely functioning. I was looking for anything that would bring me some form of peace. I went from smoking weed, to smoking cigarettes, to smoking black and milds. Drinking liquor was a norm to me. It got so bad that I had begun to drink every day, even until I would awaken with migraines. I was literally crying out for help. It was an inward cry because I was used to keeping things to myself and figuring them out on my own. I wondered if anyone could see me. Could they see this pain I was carrying and how I was losing myself trying to cover it up?

One day my mom invited me to a women's event. That day, I lay in bed tossing and turning, wavering on my decision if I should go or not. I had finally gained the strength to get up, I went, but I was late because I had gone out the night before drinking, and I had a hangover. That was the day my life began to change. I was introduced to my mentor and pastor. I didn't know it at the time, but she and all the women around me were exactly what I had needed at that very moment in my life. I remember being at the event feeling horrible that I had reeked of liquor, but no one said a thing. The enemy was encouraging me to leave, but for some reason, I felt a strong sense of peace to stay. At the end of the event, I had the opportunity to meet some amazing women who eventually became influential in my life.

After that event, it started me on a journey that I wasn't quite sure I was prepared for, but I knew that I needed more than ever because anything other than what I was doing at the time had to be better. I was walking around rejected, feeling abandoned, orphaned, and looked over. God sent people that showed me an extreme amount of love. I felt cared for around these women. I received phone calls walking me through temperance, encouraging me to go back to school to receive my degree, walking me through deliverance, showing me how to save money, teaching me how to budget my finances, how to study the word of God, how to pray, showing me what forgiveness looked like, and what a real relationship with the Father is, and I was extremely grateful. Nothing about my village was unauthentic! These women truly loved God, and it showed. Without their pour, I would have been lost. I grew in the things of God. I became a confident woman. Where there were once times I was afraid to pray, now I pray boldly, unafraid and unashamed. I refused to allow the enemy to take my voice and silence me. Where I once hid behind a mask because I didn't actually know who I was and what I really stood for, I've removed the mask because I know exactly who God has called me to be. I KNOW WHO I AM!

I began to take ministry classes, and through this ministry, I became a licensed minister. I literally have no words that can express my gratitude that the Father loves me enough to call me to serve his people in this multitude. Never in a day had I ever thought that I would be a minister of the Gospel. I had grown so much because of sisterhood and, of course, the working of the Holy Ghost. No, I wasn't perfect, and I was still overcoming things in my life, but God was doing something great, and I was blown away. This place is where I began to lead worship; my passion grew more and more each day. I began to love God, and my heart truly turned for Him; it burned for Him, and at the time, I knew that I was in the right place.

Currently, I am still in contact with the women that God put in my life when I needed them the most. But throughout my relationship with the Lord, he has blessed me with many more women. I love the women in my life dearly. I could never replace those who have helped me initially, but I absolutely adore those walking with me now. It's truly amazing what God has waiting for you on the other side. Before I needed to be discipled, but now I have the opportunity to pour into others and be the woman to them that I needed years ago today.

Bio

Alexis Ganier was born in Oak Park, Il, where her resilient and relentless mother raised her. As a leader in the local church, what she was taught as a child has certainly paid off. Alexis' ability to lead with a heart of dedication and love has allowed her to reach many people. She actively leads the singles ministry, teaches, creates, heads the worship team, participates in mentorship programs, and works alongside her Pastors. Alexis enjoys working to build and develop others, so she desired to further her education to help the youth overcome many of their obstacles and difficulties. Alexis attended National Louis University, where she got her degree in 2016. She has a Bachelor of Arts in Applied Behavioral Science. When she's not busy assisting others, she enjoys spending time with family, relaxing, watching movies, writing, learning new things, and spending time with her son Pj.

Chapter 17

A Mother's Love

- Apostle Tina M. Beatty

I remember a time in my life when the cares of this world were getting the best of me. I was becoming overwhelmed with the things I was going through in my life, it seemed like the more I tried to do right, the worse it got and the more the warfare increased.

I was dealing with hurt, rejection, fear, bitterness, sickness, betrayal, failure, unforgiveness, and disappointments, which caused me to make bad decisions in my life, and some of this that I'm talking about has nothing to do with what other people have done to me but what I thought about me. However, I was able to have a smile on my face, still preached, taught, worked, did what I knew to do, but hurting inside. I was good at hiding what I felt inside so that people around me wouldn't know what I was going through.

My Sister Helped Me Heal:

There were times when I wanted to give up on everything because I was tired of it all. As a woman, you endure so much, but to be a Woman of God in ministry, on top of that being a wife, mother, spiritual mother, grandmother, daughter, sister, aunt, cousin, friend, businesswoman, and the list can go on and on. The pressure can burden you, but I thank God for my family and a praying mother, Mrs. Tonya K. Edwards.

She has been there to pray for me through those tough times in my life. She is a special blessing. This Prayer Warrior has interceded and helped me heal in more ways than one. She has been there to love me through the pain, hurt, and every disappointment. Even when she didn't know what I was going through, she would show up out of the blue, at the right time to pray, have a scripture ready, send a card, send a text message, give me instructions, Godly wisdom and picked up food on the way to my house. It was just what I needed to bring me out of that place, to help me keep going in fulfilling my assignment. God knew what I needed to bring me out. I thank God for my mother, as well as my aunt and grandmother because you didn't just only get one, but you would get all three at different times. They all were mothers to me at different stages of my life and still are.

They helped my mother take care of me when my mother got sick with the Hồng Kong flu, which led to her having Pneumonia and then Tuberculosis. So my father and mother sent me from Yuma, Arizona, to live with my grandparents and aunt in Charleston, West Virginia, when I was 15 months old until my mother got better. So this mother's love runs deep, a generational love that only God the Father can give.

1 John 4:16, "And we have known and believed the love that God hath to us. God is love; and he that dwelleth in love dwelleth in God, and God in him." KJV

But my mother fought many battles, great and small, and this battle was great, BUT GOD can do the possible in impossible situations. But she prayed an effectual fervent prayer of faith, "Lord, heal me so that I can raise my daughter," you're talking about a mother's love.

James 5:16, "Confess your faults one to another, and pray one for another, that ye may be healed. The effectual fervent prayer of a righteous man availeth much."

But God sent me my spiritual mother to help me heal, by the name of Apostle Gloria A. McDuffey, aka Big Momma. She also knew when to call and when times were getting tough.

God knew I needed someone else in my life who would take me through deliverance so that the healing process could begin in my life. Every part of me was being affected by what was going on in my life. Apostle Gloria would tell you the truth whether you wanted to hear it or not. She didn't come to play games; she came to get you set free.

During those times, I didn't need people in my life that would agree with me while I was in that state of mind, but I needed God-sent people who knew how to war in the spirit, fast and pray, and live by the Word of God, to give me Godly wisdom and counsel, love me and not judge me but tell me the truth because I wanted to be FREE!

John 8:32, "And ye shall know the truth, and the truth shall make you free."

My mother, my spiritual mother, and others whose names aren't mentioned helped me heal and get healed the right way.

And what I mean about getting healed the right way is being healed from the inside out, not just the outside where everything looks good but healed inwardly, in my soul (mind, will, emotions) where the real fight is. I'm still fighting and overcoming every day. Apostle Paul talks about that fight in Romans 7:14-25.

There is always some part within us that we must take to the cross and lay it down because the flesh always gets in the way of our life, family, call, ministry, and assignments.

I wouldn't be the woman I am today if it wasn't for these women. God sent them into my life to hold me accountable so that I can fulfill my God-given purpose in the earth as a delivered, healed, made-whole Woman of God, as I advance the Kingdom of God, and stand before God's people, as a testimony that I Lived To Tell It, Revelation 12:11.

Bio

Apostle Tina M. Beatty is the Founder and Senior Pastor of King of Glory International Ministries and Lion of Judah International Ministries in Charleston, West Virginia. She received her Doctorate of Divinity from St. Thomas Christian University. She has an Apostolic and Prophetic call upon her life. She is the wife of Ronald C. Beatty. They have four children and six grandchildren.

She has preached for churches and conferences nationally and internationally. She is the Founder & CEO of "I LIVED TO TELL IT DELIVERANCE AND HEALING CONFERENCE." She is not ashamed to tell her testimony of how she overcame, according to Revelation 12:11.

She is an Author, Co-Author, and Entrepreneur having multiple streams of income, Nappy by Nature Salon, TMBeatty Ministries Inc., Strategic Life Coach Academy, CLS, KGU & ADS Life Institute Life Coach & Trainer, The Apostle's Closet, TMBling by the Apostle's Closet, Go Global TV, and more.

Chapter 18

Down but Not Out

- Melissa L. Bell

Growing up as the only girl and being the middle child, I was not one to have a lot of girlfriends. I had female cousins, but I was either too young or too old to truly bond with them. My mother was around, although we have never had a close relationship. When I became a mother, I did everything I thought I could possibly do to prevent the cycle from repeating itself. In some areas, I excelled, and in others, I failed miserably. As a child, I spent my time with my grandparents, usually being my grandfather's shadow. Whatever he was working on or tinkering with, I was (at the very least in my mind) his self-proclaimed assistant.

Needless to say, it took me a long time to know and understand the importance of sisterhood. I was a tomboy and really had no desire to do the "girly" things. I had to know what every power tool was, what it was used for, and how to use it. I played tackle, flag and tag football, basketball, and rode skateboards with the neighborhood boys and my older brothers' friends. It took me going through some very hard life battles to appreciate the necessity of having a trusted female voice aside from my grandmother in my life.

After the death of my grandparents at the age of 12, I was totally lost. I failed to understand why I never seemed to fit anywhere or with anyone in my youth. All of my dad's family was quiet and reserved. Not me – I was loud and talkative, almost to the point of being obnoxious. The sound of silence was irritating to me. My mother's side of the family was hundreds of miles away in other regions for the most part. So I did what most young and confused girls do, I met a boy! He told me everything a lost and neglected girl needs to hear. I was staying up late and sneaking the house out too. Before I knew it, I was a pregnant high school student and more lost than ever before.

My mother was also suffering from the loss of her adopted parents, and she fell into the pit of grief and anger. The last thing she wanted or needed in her life was to deal with a pregnant teenager. I was now in a place of being neglected by what was left of my family, and the young man also told everyone in school that he was not my baby's father. He also said he had never been intimate with me. I was completely devastated by the embarrassment that I had planned to drop out of high school in my senior year. I had no idea what I was going to do, but I refused to be the biggest joke in the building.

Upon my arrival at the Board of Education to follow through with the plan, I spoke with an elderly woman who said, "Baby, don't allow one little mistake to negatively affect you for the rest of your life. You are too smart and too pretty to let this prevent you from doing better." Once the conversation had ended, I was enrolled in home-schooling and would be able to graduate without the humiliation of the situation.

Although saved from eminent humiliation, I could not battle the depression that came with being young and having my heart broken while waging war against the hormones that were ever-changing. I had previously met three sisters at the church I attended, the Dalton girls, as we called them. Mother Dalton was a faithful member as well. The sisters saw the downward spiral, and being sisterly, they tried to help. For approximately four months, I had three sisters in my life for the first time ever! Unfortunately, they were ill-equipped for all the weight depression had dumped on me, and my stay was short-lived. I was asked to find somewhere else to go.

During the time I was with the Dalton's, I had become very close with another young lady at church. Diamond was the epitome of the perfect church girl with a little wildfire on the inside. She and her sister, Darla, the daughters of a single mother named Nina. When I told Diamond of the no longer feasible living arrangement, she spoke with her mother, Nina, and she graciously opened her door for me.

I was just entering my third trimester when I moved in. Diamond and I grew as friends and sisters. I even started getting close to her younger sister Darla too! I think I was a human form of birth control for her. For the first time in my short 17 years of life, I had a place where I fit in. Nina had traveled a long and hard road. She was not the perfect mother, but she was real. She explained life, its ups and downs, and how to ride all the points in between. She taught me how to be a young woman and how to take care of myself and not get "caught out in the world," as she put it.

If it had not been for all of the women I have mentioned here, I can only imagine how different my life would have been. I have even had to look back at some decisions and wonder if I would have a life at all. I can truly say that everything did not go perfectly with either of these situations. However, knowing that there are still good people in the world that are willing to open their doors for someone in need is a blessing that cannot be overlooked.

Diamond, Darla, and I are still lifelong friends and sisters to this day. I still call Nina, Ma, just as her biological daughters do, and she still answers. Although after 30 years we do not speak every day, we all know that family ties are not only created by blood. Bonds that are built in the face of adversity do last a lifetime.

Bio

Melissa Bell is a thought leader and administration strategist equipped professionally with over 30+ years of Customer Service Management within Fortune 500 companies. As Head of Administration for Harvest Care Ministries' Missions and Evangelism Team, she coordinated with wholesale businesses across the city to feed over a thousand hot meals, distributing bags of groceries to individuals and families in need. She organizes women retreats and multi-day ministry conferences of up to 120+, filling venues to capacity post-pandemic.

CHAPTER 19

The Drop Could Have Killed Me But God

- SHELIA COOK

The drop could have killed me but God. Ever since I can remember, I was given different narratives concerning my life and how it would turn out. Many said I would have the most children out of my mom's kids for whatever reason. Others said I wouldn't be anything, but my grandmother and my great-grandmother told me I'd be a great woman of God. It was me paying close attention to them that pulled me to a life driven by conversations with God and keeping things confidential. Before I got to that, I got dropped numerous times. The pain and frustration brought me into depression and despair that could have killed me and the ministry within me.

My Sister Helped Me Heal:

I can start by realizing I was different in so many ways that brought me rejection and pain. I was teased for being bottom-heavy. Asked by flat-chested no-butt girls if it was real. I was bullied for it a lot, so it made me self-conscious about my body make-up. This left me really depressed until I prayed not to be a girl. I prayed not to have so much body, yeah, so much body. I fought against who God created me to be because of the bullying, but it didn't stop a person I'll call Cool Breeze from molesting me or a girl I'll call Curious from touching me in a bad way. These encounters left me broken and confused about who I was and why I was here. The encounters led me to bad breakups, two divorces, and four children. These children saved my life in so many ways. Now I had ones looking up to me to be great, loving me just as I was, no one else to compare me to. I am a mom. The one and only. I poured everything in them while pushing them away at the same time, if that even makes sense. I did it to protect myself from the hurt I experienced so many times before. I was still reeling in the fact I got dropped so many times.

Then one Saturday morning, I was so tired of living a life of brokenness that I gave my life to God, cried out to him for relief, and he came, but the battle was still yet beginning. More drops, more disappointments, more confusion. The church drop was the worst because I wasn't looking for it. I had opened myself up to fully be used by God, to be in the right place at the right time to do his will. I honored church leaders to the point where I looked for them to tell me my purpose rather than let God show me first. I got dropped because of the truth I carried and told. I got blocked and told I was overzealous because of my praise. This hurt was bad; it came from all directions because I was looking for validation when God was not answering me; at least, I perceived it that way. I looked to the male leader, looked to his wife, and was getting blocked. The most hurtful thing was to be in a district meeting, and the person they had on the program wasn't there yet; I was asked to stand and proclaim in their stead. I let God lead me and was good with that. After service, I was told, "Wow, I didn't know you could do that." What a drop, this really hurt, my leaders didn't believe in me; hadn't considered me, truth be told, I hadn't considered me. Dropped, and the reality hit. I'd taken on every label placed on me and was fighting from within. This drop right here literally almost killed me but God. I decided I'd increase my prayer life and study time, not to preach or teach but to live the word of God out. My husband saw my pain, my son saw my struggle, but I kept going. I kept pushing because I really wanted things to work out where I was. I thrived on teaching in the capacity I was given knowing that I had to trust God to heal my brokenness.

I'd come home from the place of worship, the place I should have gotten healed at drained and depleted. I'd fix the Sunday dinner for my family and retreat to crying out unto the Lord. My concern was don't let the bitter root take root, but it was already there. It was eating away at my brokenness until one day God spoke to me, "I have greater for you, don't give up." This led me to ask for blinders. I wanted to just focus on God no matter what so I would gain endurance into whatever God was calling me to. Oh, but there's another drop coming. It started with a lie, but by this point, I was learning the lessons, and my ear was to the mouth of God. He let me know the drop was coming and it was okay to let it happen. I saw the lie when it was told. During service, I tried to speak up, but leadership said it was nothing they could do, dropped. I cried like a newborn baby, wept it out until I had no more tears because my character should have spoken for me; I was there before she got there. Oh, this hurt; I felt like I would die. They always declared, know them who labor among you, so why didn't you stop the lie or speak up for me? I didn't know who to trust. God led us to leave. Everyone in my family questioned my faith, but God. He turned right around and gave me a sisterhood that literally saved my life, and I'm here today because of it. I got dropped; it could have killed me, but God. I'm truly a living testimony, and I'm determined to help everyone I can walk in their God-given purpose.

Bio

I'm Rev. Shelia K. Cook, a native of Virginia Beach, Virginia resident who grew up in the Seatack area of Virginia Beach. I attended local public schools and graduated from Floyd Kellam High School. I currently hold an Associate's degree in Medical Assistance.

During my pursuance of the call, God led my family and me to Mount Olive Baptist Church in Virginia Beach, VA, under the leadership of Pastor Jason and Lady Denise Knight. I am supported in ministry by my loving husband, Deacon Craig A. Cook, our four sons, and five grandsons, along with numerous family and friends. In addition, I have written two short books to help us in our prayer life as well as in our walk in Christ titled "It's Your Time It's Personal" and "The Door Within," as well as started a ministry God's Love Covers derived from 1 Peter 4:8 during my prayer time with God.

Chapter 20

Ode to My Sisters

- Tamia Copeland

God has a way of restoring areas of brokenness in our lives. By spending more time with God, I realized that if God is who I serve, then I have to trust what He does and who He sends into my life. At times I would isolate myself in an effort to protect myself when that was God's responsibility. Being bullied as a young girl really played on my trust in God and people, and caused me to struggle with rejection. I wanted to belong with them, yet they turned on me. The very people I once found safety with were no longer safe to me. I felt like the only way to remain safe was to hide and conform to the people around me. Despite developing more in my faith journey, I wasn't operating with the identity God had given me. It took me a long time to get to a place where I could just be… without apology. But, there was a beauty in allowing myself to connect with those that God had placed in my life and in allowing myself to accept what He wanted to do within me during the transitional seasons of healing.

Sisterhood. Where do I even begin? See, for me, it was in Sisterhood that true healing began. After years of trauma and feeling like I had to endure it alone, it was the first time I could free myself and give these burdens a new home.

Bear one another's burdens, and so fulfill the law of Christ

GALATIANS 6:2 ESV

God places people in your life to do life with you, but I was so used to doing life alone that I needed a shift in perspective. I would pray for God to send me people I could connect with, but I pushed them away when they came. I blinded myself to them because of fear of what would happen if I let them in. I had to learn to trust others and myself with making the right decisions of who to connect with after seeing what happened when I previously decided to trust people. I had to learn how to trust the God within me enough to know that I was safe to confide in those He placed around me. He was safeguarding me, and in His protection, I found peace to share my story of being molested, sexually harassed, bullied, and of my struggles with depression, anxiety, self-harm, and suicidal thoughts with the first real friend I ever had. I allowed myself to be vulnerable, and for the first time, it didn't hurt me but instead allowed me to make progressive strides toward healing.

> *They placed a spiritual mirror up to my heart and helped me to see that little girl in me still resided, but I could grow beyond the trauma once I claimed the new identity God provided Therefore, if anyone is in Christ, he is a new creation. The old has passed away; behold, the new has come.*
>
> 2 CORINTHIANS 5:17 ESV

Due to the trauma I faced, I developed a flawed perspective of self. All I could see was the little girl living within me who was hurt and didn't know how to break out of that. However, I am not her anymore. I don't want people to see me through the lens of what I've been through but rather how God sees me. God placed people into my life to speak to where I was and speak to where I was going. They showed me how necessary and important I was to a world that I thought would be better off without me. They saw me through the lens of Christ and helped me to see myself as the person I truly was created as rather than the person that my trauma began to morph me into. There's something so freeing about not proving your worth to people, but rather having it acknowledged, affirmed, accepted, and appreciated.

Through the ebbs and flows of life, a new sister came in each season that came to invade the darkness of depression and anxiety, with some laughter and light.

As iron sharpens iron, so a friend sharpens a friend.

PROVERBS 27:17 NLT

Each new sister was a person of comfort that made sure I didn't get stuck in comfortability but instead pushed me past it. They did life with me and thought like me, but also challenged me by initiating intentional conversations and asking questions that helped to shape and mold me into everything I could potentially be. It was imperative for me to surround myself with people who were connected to and rooted in God. They loved me with His love and reminded me of His truth when I seemed to forget. Even when they didn't have words to say, they would intercede for me. Beyond the words of comfort and encouragement they could share with me, they chose to give God, the one who could actually change and fix my situations, an invitation into them. They actually walked alongside me on the journey of growth and helped me to get to where I needed to be.

They even offered a safe place for me to rest when I became weary of trying to outrun the shadow that followed behind me.

Then Jesus said, "*Come* to me, *all* of you *who are weary* and carry heavy burdens, and I will give you rest.

Matthew 11:28 NLT

Despite feeling misunderstood for so long, God placed kingdom sisters on my path that would embrace all that I was. I made sense to them. I finally felt like I could rest my weary wings, which I had always wanted. I belonged and finally found safety with people who didn't see me as a threat or a bother, but saw me as a friend, a confidant, and a sister.

Bio

Tamia Denise Copeland boldly and passionately uses creative expression, her God-given wit, and compassion to remind people of their worth. Though once feeling called and compelled to entrepreneurship, she realized that her greater passion and call was to partner with God through her entrepreneurial ventures to bridge the gap between God, the lost, and the brokenhearted. She's a vessel used to help people identify, embrace, and operate in their God-given identity. Being an all-around creative who desires to inspire, encourage, and motivate others to share their personal story to produce purpose out of pain, she lives to serve God and others well. She desires to create a safe space for people to connect and feel accepted not because of what they do but simply for who they are. She meets people where they are in hopes of pushing them further to where they're destined to be.

Epilogue

This is Just Our Beginning

As I read the pages that you have enjoyed before getting to this final cataclysmic moment, I know there were moments you felt the words jumping off the page. I knew there were moments you "saw" yourself telling your same story almost.

Each of these women made a courageous and bold step not just for themselves but for the women who helped them live, grow, mature, and even keep living another day to fulfill a purpose that is just beginning to unfold.

What is your story, sis? What has God done in your life, and how impactful were the sisters, and who were alongside you on that journey? Me? It was absolutely necessary for God to send me and show me the power and the love he had for me even through sisterhood- but not just any sisterhood- kingdom sisterhood.

Molested, rejected, abandoned, depressed, bitter, angry, resentful, masked, confused, overlooked, overwhelmed, ostracized- all describe me in different stages of my life that I encountered hardship that could have made me abort the assignment on my life.

As women, most have the natural ability to give birth while others experience tragic and horrific challenges with conception. I am a representative of that population of women. However, no matter what challenges may be present in the natural, all women have the ability to give birth in the spirit.

When we help another sister heal, we become midwives in their birthing process. As ones who have gone through their own healing process, they know to coach other women to do the same.

I've heard giving birth for the first time can be very scary, but the reality is the same possible dangers of birthing the first child are still present with the next.

Some women have not given birth at all yet, and there are others who are birthing again. Life's challenges are often the contractions that are just signs of what you carry.

Sis, dont underestimate yourself another day; don't "believe the" lie that you dont have the power to be the midwife for someone else. Finally, sis, don't hide the pain you had to endure to be who you are and do what God has called you to do.

I am thankful for the tribe of women God brought into my life to help me heal from brokenness, old mindsets, guilt, fear, shame, and so much more.

In 2019, Real Talk Kim Live at 9 pm caused me to get out of depression, with all the challenges of life and marriage. In 2020, it was Dr. Dean and Destiny Inspire who helped me to destroy limiting belief systems and walk in purpose confidently. Also, Bianca Brown was a person that literally spoke life into me as a branding specialist. She spoke the global call on my life when I thought maybe it was not for me because things were not moving at the rate I thought.

In the years before 2019 and sometime after were these ladies who helped me heal:

My Sister Helped Me Heal:

Lakia Perez, Kiyanni Bryan, Shelia Cook, Ciara Mason, Melissa Daughtry, Sudena Nicole, Apostle Michelle Franklin, Dr. Karen Hills Pruden, Prophetess Deleigh Ryan, Sharmela Christmon, Domonique Peele, Annie Nimley, Pastor Wendy Whitaker, Kristal Klear, Jomeica Fenner, Shaneice Jones, Lashanay Knight, Kim Brooks, Apostle Bianca Lowry, and many more.

My heart is happy because together, we break the stigma of women being unable to collaborate. Through the power of prayer, encouragement, and love, our sisters helped us heal!

Thank you for reading. I pray God heals your heart completely, and he sends sisters your way to help you live and give birth to your purpose.

www.ingramcontent.com/pod-product-compliance
Lightning Source LLC
Chambersburg PA
CBHW050916160426
43194CB00011B/2428